CONTENTS

SCANTY PLOT OF GROUND

also by Paul Muldoon

poetry
NEW WEATHER
MULES
WHY BROWNLEE LEFT
QUOOF
MEETING THE BRITISH
SELECTED POEMS 1968–1983
MADOC: A MYSTERY
THE ANNALS OF CHILE
NEW SELECTED POEMS 1968–1994
HAY
BANDANNA
POEMS 1968–1998
MOY SAND AND GRAVEL
HORSE LATITUDES
MAGGOT
THE WORD ON THE STREET: ROCK LYRICS
ONE THOUSAND THINGS WORTH KNOWING
SELECTED POEMS 1968–2014
FROLIC AND DETOUR
HOWDIE-SKELP
JOY IN SERVICE ON RUE TAGORE

prose
TO IRELAND I: AN ABECEDARY OF IRISH LITERATURE
THE END OF THE POEM: OXFORD LECTURES IN POETRY

editor
CONTEMPORARY IRISH POETRY
THE FABER BOOK OF BEASTS
LORD BYRON: SELECTED POEMS
JOHN DONNE: SELECTED POEMS

for children
THE LAST THESAURUS
THE NOCTUARY OF NARCISSUS BATT

SCANTY PLOT OF GROUND
A BOOK OF SONNETS

EDITED BY
PAUL MULDOON

faber

First published in 2025
by Faber & Faber Ltd
The Bindery, 51 Hatton Garden
London, EC1N 8HN

Typeset by Typo•glyphix, Burton-on-Trent, DE14 3HE
Printed in the UK by Short Run Press

Cover typeface: DT World Tour Font
© Nurjannah Suhaimi / Death by Typography

A CIP record for this book
is available from the British Library

ISBN 978–0–571–37344–4

MIX
Paper | Supporting
responsible forestry
FSC® C014540

Printed and bound in the UK on FSC® certified paper in line with our continuing
commitment to ethical business practices, sustainability and the environment.
For further information see faber.co.uk/environmental-policy

Our authorised representative in the EU for product safety is
Easy Access System Europe, Mustamäe tee 50, 10621 Tallinn, Estonia
gpsr.requests@easproject.com

2 4 6 8 10 9 7 5 3 1

INTRODUCTION

Of the innumerable traditional verse forms, the sonnet is not only the most persistent but also the most pervasive. As Carl Phillips has reminded us, its persistence has to do with its near indestructability:

> The sonnet has a greater tolerance for innovation – while retaining its essential formal structure – than do many fixed forms . . . The sonnet is always recognizable, despite the innovation. You can remove the rhyme, the meter of a sonnet, and it's still possible to retain the sonnet's mode of delivery of information, its logic, its argumentation. This isn't so for the villanelle or sestina, for example. Nor for the limerick. Nor for the rondeau.

The pervasive aspect of the sonnet – its widespread occurrence – may be explained partly by its comparatively complex origin story. The generally accepted theory is that we first encounter it at the court of the Holy Roman Emperor Frederick II from the thirteenth-century Sicilian poet Giacomo da Lentini, who seems to have taken the *strambotto*, an eight-line stanza rhyming *abab abab* hitherto used in Sicilian songs, and promptly added a sestet. Some scholars claim that other, deeper, sources may be the Arabic *muwashshah*, which had developed in Muslim Spain in the eleventh and twelfth centuries, as well as verse forms (also of Arabic origin), associated with French and

Spanish troubadours. Like an invasive species – bamboo or the American bullfrog, or the 'switchgrass beachgrass' that open Carl Phillips's sonnet, 'Invasive Species' – this 'little song' made its way from Sicily to Tuscany and became particularly associated with Francesco Petrarca (Petrarch), the author of the sequence of sonnets known as *Il Canzoniere*. Like Dante Alighieri before him, Petrarch dedicated his sonnets to a specific woman but retained within them many of the generic conventions associated with courtly love.

It was two courtiers, Sir Thomas Wyatt and Sir Henry Howard, the Earl of Surrey, who imported the form from Italy into England in the sixteenth century. The 'form' to which I refer is the Petrarchan sonnet, its rhyme scheme *abba abba cde cde*. The conventional way of thinking about this structure is that the first eight lines involve a setting down of a circumstance and the remaining six lines involve a twist on it that might include anything from a mild proviso to a blatant rebuttal. What looks to some like a lopsided relationship between the octave and sestet will appear to others as an embodiment of the Golden Ratio. Two quantities are in the golden ratio if their ratio is the same as the ratio of their sum to the larger of the two quantities. That ratio is generally given as 1.618 or, in terms of the mathematical division of a line, a ratio of 8 to 13. The golden ratio was called the 'extreme and mean ratio' by Euclid and the 'divine proportion' by Luca Pacioli, the Italian mathematician who counted among his inventions the double-entry system of bookkeeping.

The mathematical aspect of the sonnet is much to the fore in its other main manifestation, that associated with William

Shakespeare. The Shakespearean sonnet consists of three quatrains and a couplet rhyming *abab cdcd efef gg*. The effect of this final couplet is partly reminiscent of the *envoi*, the short stanza concluding a troubadour's *ballade*, but it functions mostly as a version of the Euclidean QED (*quod erat demonstrandum*) we find at the end of a theorem or mathematical proof. William Bell Scott in 'Of Poetry' puts it memorably:

> But not the less our Shakespeare knew
> Another way; by full discourse
> To show his picture as it grew,
> Worked out in many-sided force.
>
> Then when the heart can wish no more,
> With a strong couplet bars the door.

Both forms incorporate the *volta* or 'turn' – an 'often breathtakingly indefinable pivot [that] remains a vital component of the governing structure', as Christina Pugh describes in 'On Sonnet Thought'. In broad terms, the Petrarchan sonnet seems open to discussion while the Shakespearean sometimes gives the impression of a mind made up, perhaps inflexibly so.

The single most astute comment on the form in general comes from Paul Oppenheimer in his magnificent 1989 study, *The Birth of the Modern Mind: Self, Consciousness, and the Invention of the Sonnet*, where he asserts that the sonnet was:

> the first lyric form since the fall of the Roman Empire intended not for music or performance but for silent reading. As such, it is the first lyric of self-consciousness,

or of the self in conflict . . . The new form was quickly understood as a new way of thinking about mankind. Emotional problems, especially problems in love, needed no longer merely be expressed or performed: they might now actually be resolved, or provisionally resolved, through the logic of a form that turned expression inward.

The sonnet allows us the impression of observing the thought-process of the speaker of the poem to such an extent that what we're engaged with is not a poem at all but a form of drama. We are privy to a revelation that seems to be enacted in real time.

Whether it be Petrarchan or Shakespearean, hesitantly rehearsing an argument or wholeheartedly making a claim, the sonnet is sufficiently capacious to take in almost anything. The same is true of this anthology, one that by necessity presents a very partial view of a vast subject. The sonnets gathered here are first of all ones with which I have a particular connection. They do double duty, though, by giving a sense of the history of the form. While I focus on the sonnet in English, there are a few poems in translation. These include César Vallejo's 'Testimony'; Rainer Maria Rilke's 'The Unicorn'; Charles Baudelaire's mind-bending 'Correspondences'; and the scurrilous 'Arsehole' by the Zutiste tag-team of Paul Verlaine and Arthur Rimbaud – the former providing the quatrains, the latter the tercets – for their unlikely vision of a Promised Land.

The sonnets are presented alphabetically by author surname, the rationale being that the form has proved durable beyond the specifics not only of place but time. Part of the reason for that durability is the sonnet's specific duration. It's the perfect length in which to address a subject without either glossing over it or blaring on ad nauseam. Michael Theune writes tellingly of the sonnet's physical footprint, the square footage of the real estate it occupies: 'Formally, virtually every sonnet is, at least in part, a concrete poem that looks like a sonnet.' Quite apart from any aural considerations, there's no accounting for the physical impact of the poem on the page. An architectural image – of a mausoleum, perhaps? – lies behind Dante Gabriel Rossetti's succinct description in 'The Sonnet' of the form's own capacity for succinctness:

A Sonnet is a moment's monument, –
Memorial from the Soul's eternity
To one dead deathless hour.

The 'scanty plot' or close quarters of the sonnet are emphasised in William Wordsworth's 'Nuns fret not at their convent's narrow room', the 'room' referring to the 'stanza' (the Italian root of which means 'a room'). The 'fret' connects partly to an 'interlaced pattern' but is also etymologically related to a term for a 'shackle'. Imagery associated with imprisonment abounds in the sonnet in English. Although many practitioners find that the confines of the sonnet are in fact liberating, the general sense is that it's a form preoccupied with limitations. Take John Keats and his diagnostic:

If by dull rhymes our English must be chain'd,
And, like Andromeda, the sonnet sweet
Fetter'd . . .

At the heart of 'If We Must Die' by Claude McKay is the image of being 'penned', 'constrained' and 'pressed to the wall'. The word 'penned' is particularly evocative, since it summons up both the Federal Penitentiary and the pen that may indeed be mightier than the sword. In his groundbreaking *The African American Sonnet: A Literary History*, Timo Müller points out that:

> African American poets evoked the boundedness of the sonnet not so much to assert national or cultural belonging, as to trouble the limitations such concepts imply.

Take Wanda Coleman and her ambition that her 'American sonnet' be:

> as open as possible, adhering only to the loosely followed dictate of number of lines. I decided on 14 to 16 and to not exceed that, but to go absolutely bonkers within that constraint.

For Terrance Hayes, the revamped 'American sonnet' that he inherited from Coleman may indeed be 'part prison' but it is a prison with a recreation yard – perhaps even a sequence of interconnected recreation yards. A number of Black poets have risen to the challenge of the sonnet cycle (including the 'crown' of sonnets) that has exercised many, from Lady Mary Wroth to Edna St Vincent Millay. This edition features examples from 'A Wreath for Emmett Till' by Marilyn Nelson and 'House of Unending' by Reginald Dwayne Betts, among others. The title 'House of Unending' hints at the idea of continuity in the sonnet tradition that reflects the perpetual conversation between poems from different eras and different traditions – as testified by this anthology with its wide-ranging gathering of voices.

The ongoing capacity of the sonnet to allow for both chaos and control is one that will ensure its viability even in our increasingly fractious and factional of times. The sonnet is supremely well adapted to allowing for the related phenomena of grave restraint and giddy release. It is accommodating while insisting on a few basic house rules. It is a room which we may make our own while being simultaneously mindful of, and oblivious to, the other guests who have occupied it over the centuries.

PAUL MULDOON, 2025

REFERENCES

Carl Phillips, 'Whose Sonnet?: (A Transgression)', *The American Sonnet: An Anthology of Poems and Essays*, eds Dora Malech and Laura T. Smith (University of Iowa Press, 2022)

Christina Pugh, 'On Sonnet Thought', *Literary Imagination*, Volume 12, Issue 3 (2010)

Paul Oppenheimer, *The Birth of the Modern Mind: Self, Consciousness, and the Invention of the Sonnet* (Oxford University Press, 1989)

Michael Theune, 'Strange Voltas', *The American Sonnet: An Anthology of Poems and Essays*, eds Dora Malech and Laura T. Smith (University of Iowa Press, 2022)

Timo Müller, *The African American Sonnet: A Literary History* (University Press of Mississippi, 2018)

Wanda Coleman, 'American Sonnets' email interview with Paul E. Nelson (2008): https://paulenelson.com/workshops/wanda-coleman-american-sonnets/

SCANTY PLOT OF GROUND

In a Spring Grove

Here the white-ray'd anemone is born,
Wood-sorrel, and the varnish'd buttercup;
And primrose in its purfled green swathed up,
Pallid and sweet round every budding thorn,
Gray ash, and beech with rusty leaves outworn.
Here, too, the darting linnet hath her nest
In the blue-lustred holly, never shorn,
Whose partner cheers her little brooding breast,
Piping from some ncar bough. O simple song!
O cistern deep of that harmonious rillet,
And these fair juicy stems that climb and throng
The vernal world, and unexhausted seas
Of flowing life, and soul that asks to fill it,
Each and all of these,—and more, and more than these!

Shakespeare

Others abide our question. Thou art free.
We ask and ask. Thou smilest and art still,
Out-topping knowledge. For the loftiest hill
Who to the stars uncrowns his majesty,
Planting his steadfast footsteps in the sea,
Making the heaven of heavens his dwelling-place,
Spears but the cloudy border of his base
To the foiled searching of mortality.
And thou, who didst the stars and sunbeams know,
Self-schooled, self-scanned, self-honoured, self-secure,
Didst tread on earth unguessed at. Better so!
All pains the immortal spirit must endure,
All weakness which impairs, all griefs which bow,
Find their sole speech in that victorious brow.

W. H. AUDEN

The Traveller

No window in his suburb lights that bedroom where
A little fever heard large afternoons at play:
His meadows multiply; that mill, though, is not there
Which went on grinding at the back of love all day.

Nor all his weeping ways through weary wastes have found
The castle where his Greater Hallows are interned;
For broken bridges halt him, and dark thickets round
Some ruin where an evil heritage was burned.

Could he forget a child's ambition to be old
And institutions where it learned to wash and lie,
He'd tell the truth for which he thinks himself too young,

That everywhere on his horizon of his sigh
Is now, as always, only waiting to be told
To be his father's house and speak his mother tongue.

PHILIP AYRES

Cynthia on Horseback

Fair Cynthia mounted on her sprightly pad,
Which in white robe with silver fringe was clad,
    And swift as wind his graceful steps did move,
    As with his beauteous guide he'd been in love.

Though fierce, yet humble still to her command,
Obeying every touch of her fair hand;
    Her golden bit his foaming mouth did check,
    It spread his crest, and raised his bending neck.

She was the rose upon this hill of snow,
Her sparkling beauty made the glorious show
    Whence secret flames men in their bosoms took.
The graces and the cupids her surround,
Attending her, while cruel she does wound
    With switch her horse, and hearts with every look.

CHARLES BAUDELAIRE
Correspondences

Nature itself is a temple in which these living columns
may manage what some will take for speech;
we pass through a forest of symbol-laden ash or beech
that glimpses us no less knowingly than we glimpse

how echoes, far-off, reverberate with a renewed verve
in a Oneness both pitch dark and profound,
boundless as night, or daylight without bounds,
its perfumes, colors, and sounds in a back-and-forth.

Some of those perfumes are sweet as a baby's pelt,
oboe-bright, green to that distant horizon;
others are quite funky, fly-blown, beating a big drum,

building as all illimitable things must build –
the amber, musk, frankincense, and gum resin
giving voice to the soul's throb as to the body's thrum.

translated by Paul Muldoon

To My Mother

Most near, most dear, most loved and most far,
Under the window where I often found her
Sitting as huge as Asia, seismic with laughter,
Gin and chicken helpless in her Irish hand,
Irresistible as Rabelais, but most tender for
The lame dogs and hurt birds that surround her,—
She is a procession no one can follow after
But be like a little dog following a brass band.

She will not glance up at the bomber, or condescend
To drop her gin and scuttle to a cellar,
But lean on the mahogany table like a mountain
Whom only faith can move, and so I send
O all my faith, and all my love to tell her
That she will move from mourning into morning.

APHRA BEHN

Epitaph on the Tombstone of a Child, the last of Seven that died before

This little, silent, gloomy monument
Contains all that was sweet and innocent,
The softest prattler that e'er found a tongue.
His voice was music and his words a song,
Which now each listening angel smiling hears,
Such pretty harmonies compose the spheres.
Wanton as unfledged cupids, ere their charms
Had learned the little arts of doing harms,
Fair as young cherubins, as soft and kind,
And though translated could not be refined,
The seventh dear pledge the nuptial joys had given,
Toiled here on earth, retired to rest in heaven,
Where they the shining host of angels fill,
Spread their gay wings before the throne, and smile.

JOHN BERRYMAN

Sonnet 13

I lift—lift you five States away your glass,
Wide of this bar you never graced, where none
Ever I know came, where what work is done
Even by these men I know not, where a brass
Police-car sign peers in, wet strange cars pass,
Soiled hangs the rag of day out over this town,
A juke-box brains air where I drink alone,
The spruce barkeep sports a toupee alas—

My glass I lift at six o'clock, my darling,
As you plotted . . Chinese couples shift in bed,
We shared today not even filthy weather,
Beasts in the hills their tigerish love are snarling,
Suddenly they clash, I blow my short ash red,
Grey eyes light! and we have our drink together.

House of Unending

I

The sinner's bouquet, house of shredded & torn
   Dear John letters, upended grave of names, moon
      Black kiss of a pistol's flat side, time blueborn
& threaded into a curse, Lazarus of hustlers, the picayune
Spinning into beatdown; breath of a thief stilled
      By fluorescent lights, a system of 40 blocks,
      Empty vials, a hand full of purple cranesbills,
Memories of crates suspended from stairs, tied in knots
Around streetlamps, the house of unending push-ups,
      Wheelbarrows & walking 20s, the daughters
      Chasing their fathers' shadows, sons that upset
The wind with their secrets, the paraphrase of fractured,
      Scarred wings flying through smoke, each wild hour
      Of lockdown, hunger time & the blackened flower.

Of lockdown, hunger time & the blackened flower—
    Ain't nothing worth knowing. Prison becomes home;
The cell: a catacomb that cages and the metronome
    Tracking the years that eclipse you. History authors

Your death, throws you into that din of lost hours.
    Your mother blames it all on your X chromosome,
Blames it on something in the blood, a Styrofoam
Cup filled with whiskey leading you to court disfavor,

To become drunk on count-time & chow-call logic.
    There is no name for this thing that you've become:
Convict, hostage, inmate, lifer, yardbird, all fail.
    If you can't be free, be a mystery. An amnesic.
Anything. But avoid succumbing to the humdrum:
Swallowing a bullet or even just choosing to inhale.

Swallowing a bullet or even just choosing to inhale,
    Both mark you: pistol or the blunt to the head
Escorting you through the night. Your Yale—
    An omen, the memories, the depression, the dead

And how things keep getting in the way of things.
When he asked you for the pistol, and you said no,
    The reluctance wasn't about what violence brings.
His weeping in your ear made you regret what you owed.

On some days, the hard ones, you curse the phone,
    The people calling collect, reaching out, all buried,
Surrounded by bricks. On some days, you've known
You wouldn't answer, the blinking numbers as varied

As the names of the prisons holding on to those lives,
Holding on, ensuring that nothing survives.

4

Holding on, ensuring that nothing survives,
Not even regret. That's the thing that gets you,
Holding on to memories like they're your archives,
   Like they're there to tell you something true

About what happened. My past put a skew
   On how I held her. Unaccustomed to touch,
I knew only dream & fantasy. Try to see through
That mire and find intimacy. It was just so much.

   & then, the yesterdays just become yesterday,
A story that you tell yourself about not dying,
Another thing, when it's mentioned, to downplay.
That's what me and that woman did, trying

To love each other. What kind of fool am I,
Lost in what's gone, reinventing myself with lies.

5

Lost in what's gone, reinventing myself with lies:
I walk these streets, ruined by what I'd hide.
Jesus died for somebody's sins, but not mine.

I barely see my daughters at all these days.
    Out here caught up, lost in an old cliché.
But tell me, what won't these felonies betray?

Did a stretch in prison to be released to a cell.
    Returned to a freedom penned by Orwell.
My noon temptation is now the Metro's third rail.

In my wallet, I carry around my daguerreotype,
    A mugshot, no smiles, my name a tithe.
What must I pay for being this stereotype?

The pistols I carried into the night, my anchor;
The crimes that unraveled me, my banner.

6

The crimes that unraveled me—my banner.
  Only a fool confesses to owning that fact.
Honesty a sinkhole; the truth doomed to subtract
Everything but prayer, turn my breath into failure.

  Whiskey after prison made me crave amber,
Brown washing my glass until I'm smacked.
  The murder of crows on my arm an artifact
    Of freedom: what outlasts even the jailor.

  Alas, there is no baptism for me tonight.
No water to drown all these memories.
  The rooms in my head keep secrets that indict
Me still; my chorus of unspoken larcenies.

  You carry that knowledge into your twilight,
& live without regret for your guilty pleas.

& live without regret for your guilty pleas—
    Shit. Mornings I rise twice: once for a count
That will not come & later with the city's
    Wild birds, who find freedom without counsel.

I left prison with debts no honest man could pay.
    Walked out imagining I'd lapped my troubles,
but a girl once said no to my closed ears, dismayed
    that I didn't pause. Remorse can't calm those evils.

    I've lost myself in some kind of algebra
That turns my life into an equation that zeroes
    Out, regardless of my efforts. Algophobia
Means to fear pain. I still fear who knows

    All I've done. Why regret this thing I've worn?
The sinner's bouquet; house, shredded & torn.

ELIZABETH BISHOP
Some Dreams They Forgot

The dead birds fell, but no one had seen them fly,
or could guess from where. They were black, their eyes were shut,
and no one knew what kind of birds they were. But
all held them and looked up through the new far-funneled sky.
Also, dark drops fell. Night-collected on the eaves,
or congregated on the ceilings over their beds,
they hung, mysterious drop-shapes, all night over their heads,
now rolling off their careless fingers quick as dew off leaves.
Where had they seen wood-berries perfect black as these,
shining just so in early morning? Dark-hearted decoys on
upper-bough or below-leaf. Had they thought *poison*
and left? or—remember—eaten them from the loaded trees?
What flowers shrink to seeds like these, like columbine?
But their dreams are all inscrutable by eight or nine.

If it is true, what the Prophets write

If it is true, what the Prophets write,
That the heathen gods are all stocks and stones,
Shall we, for the sake of being polite,
Feed them with the juice of our marrow-bones?

And if Bezaleel and Aholiab drew
What the finger of God pointed to their view,
Shall we suffer the Roman and Grecian rods
To compel us to worship them as gods?

They stole them from the temple of the Lord
And worshipp'd them that they might make inspirèd art abhorr'd;

The wood and stone were call'd the holy things,
And their sublime intent given to their kings.
All the atonements of Jehovah spurn'd,
And criminals to sacrifices turn'd.

WILFRID SCAWEN BLUNT
The Deeds That Might Have Been

There are wrongs done in the fair face of heaven
Which cry aloud for vengeance, and shall cry;
Loves beautiful in strength whose wit has striven
Vainly with loss and man's inconstancy;
Dead children's faces watched by souls that die;
Pure streams defiled; fair forests idly riven;
A nation suppliant in its agony
Calling on justice, and no help is given.

All these are pitiful. Yet, after tears,
Come rest and sleep and calm forgetfulness,
And God's good providence consoles the years.
Only the coward heart which did not guess,
The dreamer of brave deeds that might have been,
Shall cureless ache with wounds forever green.

The Soldier

If I should die, think only this of me:
   That there's some corner of a foreign field
That is for ever England. There shall be
   In that rich earth a richer dust concealed;
A dust whom England bore, shaped, made aware,
   Gave, once, her flowers to love, her ways to roam,
A body of England's, breathing English air,
   Washed by the rivers, blest by suns of home.

And think, this heart, all evil shed away,
   A pulse in the eternal mind, no less
      Gives somewhere back the thoughts by England given;
Her sights and sounds; dreams happy as her day;
   And laughter, learnt of friends; and gentleness,
      In hearts at peace, under an English heaven.

GWENDOLYN BROOKS
Mentors

For I am rightful fellow of their band.
My best allegiances are to the dead.
I swear to keep the dead upon my mind,
Disdain for all time to be overglad.
Among spring flowers, under summer trees,
By chilling autumn waters, in the frosts
Of supercilious winter—all my days
I'll have as mentors those reproving ghosts.
And at that cry, at that remotest whisper,
I'll stop my casual business. Leave the banquet.
Or leave the ball—reluctant to unclasp her
Who may be fragrant as the flower she wears,
Make gallant bows and dim excuses, then quit
Light for the midnight that is mine and theirs.

ELIZABETH BARRETT BROWNING

from *Sonnets from the Portuguese*

43

How do I love thee? Let me count the ways.
I love thee to the depth and breadth and height
My soul can reach, when feeling out of sight
For the ends of Being and ideal Grace.
I love thee to the level of everyday's
Most quiet need, by sun and candle-light.
I love thee freely, as men strive for Right;
I love thee purely, as they turn from Praise.
I love thee with the passion put to use
In my old griefs, and with my childhood's faith.
I love thee with a love I seemed to lose
With my lost saints, —I love thee with the breath,
Smiles, tears, of all my life! —and, if God choose,
I shall but love thee better after death.

ROBERT BROWNING

Misconceptions

I

This is a spray the Bird clung to,
  Making it blossom with pleasure,
Ere the high tree-top she sprung to,
  Fit for her nest and her treasure.
  Oh, what a hope beyond measure
Was the poor spray's, which the flying feet hung to,—
So to be singled out, built in, and sung to!

II

This is a heart the Queen leant on,
  Thrilled in a minute erratic,
Ere the true bosom she bent on,
  Meet for love's regal dalmatic.
  Oh, what a fancy ecstatic
Was the poor heart's, ere the wanderer went on—
Love to be saved for it, proffered to, spent on!

WILLIAM CULLEN BRYANT
Sonnet—Mutation

They talk of short-lived pleasure—be it so—
Pain dies as quickly: stern, hard-featured pain
Expires, and lets her weary prisoner go.
The fiercest agonies have shortest reign;
And after dreams of horror, comes again
The welcome morning with its rays of peace.
Oblivion, softly wiping out the stain,
Makes the strong secret pangs of shame to cease:
Remorse is virtue's root; its fair increase
Are fruits of innocence and blessedness:
Thus joy, o'erborne and bound, doth still release
His young limbs from the chains that round him press.
Weep not that the world changes—did it keep
A stable changeless state, 'twere cause indeed to weep.

ROBERT BURNS
A Sonnet upon Sonnets

Fourteen, a sonneteer thy praises sings;
What magic myst'ries in that number lie!
Your hen hath fourteen eggs beneath her wings
That fourteen chickens to the roost may fly.
Fourteen full pounds the jockey's stone must be;
His age fourteen – a horse's prime is past.
Fourteen long hours too oft the Bard must fast;
Fourteen bright bumpers – bliss he ne'er must see!
Before fourteen, a dozen yields the strife;
Before fourteen – e'en thirteen's strength is vain.
Fourteen good years – a woman gives us life;
Fourteen good men – we lose that life again.
What lucubrations can be more upon it?
Fourteen good measur'd verses make a sonnet.

Mediocrity in Love Rejected

Give me more love or more disdain;
The torrid, or the frozen zone,
Bring equal ease unto my pain;
The temperate affords me none;
Either extreme, of love, or hate,
Is sweeter than a calm estate.

Give me a storm; if it be love,
Like Danae in that golden show'r
I swim in pleasure; if it prove
Disdain, that torrent will devour
My vulture-hopes; and he's possess'd
Of heaven, that's but from hell releas'd.

Then crown my joys, or cure my pain;
Give me more love, or more disdain.

Spenser's Ireland

Rakehelly horseboys, kernes, gallowglasses, carrows,
Bards, captains, rapparees, their forward womenfolk,
Swords, dice, whiskey, chess, harps, word-hoards, bows and arrows:
All are hid within the foldings of their Irish cloak.

Fit house for an outlaw, meet bed for a rebel,
This whore's wardrobe is convenient for a thief;
And when it freezes it becomes his tabernacle,
In whose snug he finds Hibernian relief.

Then there is this big thick bush of hair hanging down
Over their eyes—a *glib*, they call it in their spake;
They do not recognize the power of the Crown.

At the drop of a hat they are wont to vanish
Into deep dark woods. Forever on the make,
They drink and talk too much. Not all of it is gibberish.

GEORGE CHAPMAN
Sonnet to the Countess of Bedford

To you, faire Patronesse, and Muse to Learning;
The Fount of learning and the Muses sends
This Cordiall for your vertues; and forewarning
To leaue no good, for th'ill the world commends.
Custome seduceth but the vulgar sort:
With whom, when Noblesse mixeth, she is vulgare;
The truly-Noble, still repaire their Fort,
With gracing good excitements, and gifts rare;
In which the narrow path, to Happinesse,
Is onely beaten. Vulgar pleasure sets
Nets for her selfe, in swinge of her excesse;
And beates her selfe there dead, ere free she gets.
Since pleasure then with pleasure still doth waste;
Still please with vertue Madame: That will last.

MARILYN CHIN

Advice (for E)

Be the stealth   between stones
    The abracadabra   amongst   clones

Be the fighting fish with a fancy tail
    The wizard who   deifies   gnomes

No worry   be happy   missiles flying
    While innocents   are dying

You're pretty nimble   for your age
    One day a wombat   next day   a sage

On the way to feeding a despot
    You summoned   your rage

Most virtuous mother   don't be fooled
    They will bomb our shelter   scorch our earth

Unwind   regroup   turn swine   into pearl
    Be the change   you wanna see   in the girl

The Shepherd Boy

Pleased in his loneliness, he often lies,
    Telling glad stories to his dog or e'en
His very shadow, that the loss supplies
    Of living company. Full oft he'll lean
By pebbled brooks and dream with happy eyes
    Upon the fairy pictures spread below,
Thinking the shadowed prospects real skies
    And happy heavens where his kindred go.
Oft we may track his haunts, where he hath been
    To spend the leisure which his toils bestow,
By nine-peg morris nicked upon the green,
    Or flower-stuck gardens, never meant to grow,
    Or figures cut on trees, his skill to show,
Where he a prisoner from a shower hath been.

WANDA COLEMAN
Put Some Sex Sonnet

after Tom Clark

the honeypot becomes so sweet under his tongue
it strengthens his arousal and at the same
time causes him to lick harder, which stimulates
her further richness to facilitate a mounting
moistness. her orgasm fairly pulls him under as he
thrills to the duet of sphincter & cervix—
the inexpressible pleasure of her contractions
inspired by him—as she melds beyond complete relaxation
in too exquisite a surrender, her body opened and
well-lubricated, welcoming the easy thrust of his hips
in a spell of satisfaction, knowing yet another wave
of pleasure awaits her as his penis glides/rides
the residuals of her first wave, daring her. more

Composed on a journey homeward; the author having received intelligence of the birth of a son, Sept. 20, 1796

Oft o'er my brain does that strange fancy roll
   Which makes the present (while the flash doth last)
   Seem a mere semblance of some unknown past,
Mixed with such feelings, as perplex the soul
Self-questioned in her sleep; and some have said
   We lived, ere yet this robe of flesh we wore.
   O my sweet baby! when I reach my door,
If heavy looks should tell me thou art dead,
(As sometimes, through excess of hope, I fear)
I think that I should struggle to believe
   Thou wert a spirit, to this nether sphere
Sentenced for some more venial crime to grieve;
Did'st scream, then spring to meet Heaven's quick reprieve,
   While we wept idly o'er thy little bier!

Sonnet

All we need is fourteen lines, well, thirteen now,
and after this one just a dozen
to launch a little ship on love's storm-tossed seas,
then only ten more left like rows of beans.
How easily it goes unless you get Elizabethan
and insist the iambic bongos must be played
and rhymes positioned at the ends of lines,
one for every station of the cross.
But hang on here while we make the turn
into the final six where all will be resolved,
where longing and heartache will find an end,
where Laura will tell Petrarch to put down his pen,
take off those crazy medieval tights,
blow out the lights, and come at last to bed.

To Mary Unwin

Mary! I want a lyre with other strings,
Such aid from Heaven as some have feigned they drew,
An eloquence scarce given to mortals, new
And undebased by praise of meaner things;
That ere through age or woe I shed my wings,
I may record thy worth with honour due,
In verse as musical as thou art true,
And that immortalises whom it sings:
But thou hast little need. There is a Book
By seraphs writ with beams of heavenly light,
On which the eyes of God not rarely look,
A chronicle of actions just and bright—
    There all thy deeds, my faithful Mary, shine;
    And since thou own'st that praise, I spare thee mine.

COUNTEE CULLEN
Yet Do I Marvel

I doubt not God is good, well-meaning, kind,
And did He stoop to quibble could tell why
The little buried mole continues blind,
Why flesh that mirrors Him must some day die,
Make plain the reason tortured Tantalus
Is baited by the fickle fruit, declare
If merely brute caprice dooms Sisyphus
To struggle up a never-ending stair.
Inscrutable His ways are, and immune
To catechism by a mind too strewn
With petty cares to slightly understand
What awful brain compels His awful hand.
Yet do I marvel at this curious thing:
To make a poet black, and bid him sing!

SAMUEL DANIEL
from *Delia*

39

Read in my face a volume of despairs,
The wailing Iliads of my tragic woe;
Drawn with my blood, and printed with my cares,
Wrought by her hand, that I have honour'd so.
Who whilst I burn, she sings at my soul's wrack,
Looking aloft from turret of her pride:
There my soul's tyrant joys her, in the sack
Of her own seat, whereof I made her guide.
There do these smokes that from affliction rise,
Serve as an incense to a cruel dame:
A sacrifice thrice grateful to her eyes,
Because their power serve to'exact the same.
Thus ruins she, to satisfy her will;
The temple, where her name was honour'd still.

ELIZABETH DARYUSH
Still-Life

Through the open french window, the warm sun
lights up the polished breakfast-table, laid
round a bowl of crimson roses, for one –
a service of Worcester porcelain, arrayed
near it a melon, peaches, figs, small hot
rolls in a napkin, fairy rack of toast,
butter in ice, high silver coffee pot,
and, heaped on a salver, the morning's post.

She comes over the lawn, the young heiress,
from her early walk in her garden-wood
feeling that life's a table set to bless
her delicate desires with all that's good,

that even the unopened future lies
like a love-letter, full of sweet surprise.

SIR JOHN DAVIES

If you would know the love which I you bear

If you would know the love which I you bear,
Compare it to the Ring which your fair hand
Shall make more precious when you shall it wear:
So my love's nature you shall understand.
Is it of metal pure? so you shall prove
My love, which ne'er disloyal thought did stain.
Hath it no end? so endless is my love,
Unless you it destroy with your disdain.
Doth it the purer wax the more 'tis tried?
So doth my love: yet herein they dissent,
That whereas gold, the more 'tis purified,
By waxing less doth show some part is spent,
My love doth wax more pure by your more trying,
And yet increaseth in the purifying.

JOHN DONNE
from *Holy Sonnets*

Death be not proud

Death be not proud, though some have called thee
Mighty and dreadful, for, thou art not so,
For, those, whom thou think'st, thou dost overthrow,
Die not, poor Death, nor yet canst thou kill me;
From rest and sleep, which but thy pictures be,
Much pleasure, then from thee, much more must flow,
And soonest our best men with thee do go,
Rest of their bones, and soul's delivery.
Thou art slave to fate, chance, kings, and desperate men,
And dost with poison, war, and sickness dwell,
And poppy, or charms can make us sleep as well,
And better than thy stroke; why swell'st thou then?
One short sleep past, we wake eternally,
And death shall be no more, Death thou shalt die.

Found Sonnet: The Wig

100% human hair, natural; Yaki synthetic, Brazilian blend,
Malaysian, Kanekalon, Peruvian Virgin, Pure Indian;
iron-friendly, heat-resistant; bounce, volume, featherweight,
Short 'n' Sassy, Swirls & Twirls, Smooth & Sleek and Sleek & Straight,

Wet and Wavy, Futura fibre, weave-a-wig or Shake-n-Go;
classic, trendy, micro-kink; frosted pixie, tight cornrow;
full, three-quarter, half, stretch cap, drawstring, ear tabs, combs;
chignon, headband, clip-in bangs; easy extensions and ponytail domes—

long or bobbed, hand-tied, layered, deep twist bulk, prestyled updo,
Remi closure, Swiss lace front, invisible L part, J part, U;
feathered, fringed, extended neck; tousled, spiky, loose cascades,
sideswept, flipped ends, corkscrews, spirals, Rasta dreads, Ghana braids;

Passion Wave, Silk Straight, Faux Mohawk, Nubian locks, Noble Curl:
Cleopatra, Vintage Vixen, Empress, Hera, Party Girl.

MICHAEL DRAYTON
Since There's No Help

Since there's no help, come, let us kiss and part,
Nay, I have done: you get no more of me,
And I am glad, yea, glad with all my heart,
That thus so cleanly I myself can free;
  Shake hands forever, cancel all our vows,
And when we meet at any time again,
Be it not seen in either of our brows,
That we one jot of former love retain.
  Now at the last gasp of Love's latest breath,
When, his pulse failing, Passion speechless lies,
When Faith is kneeling by his bed of death,
And Innocence is closing up his eyes,
    Now if thou wouldst, when all have given him over,
    From death to life thou might'st him yet recover.

The Baptist

The last and greatest herald of heaven's king,
Girt with rough skins, hies to the deserts wild,
Among that savage brood the woods forth bring,
Which he than man more harmless found and mild;
His food was locusts and what there doth spring,
With honey that from virgin hives distilled;
Parched body, hollow eyes, some uncouth thing
Made him appear, long since from earth exiled.
There burst he forth: 'All ye whose hopes rely
On God, with me amidst these deserts mourn,
Repent! Repent! and from old errors turn.'
Who listened to his voice? obeyed his cry?
Only the echoes which he made relent,
Rung from their flinty caves, 'Repent! Repent!'

Anne Hathaway

Item I gyve unto my wief my second best bed . . .
FROM SHAKESPEARE'S WILL

The bed we loved in was a spinning world
of forests, castles, torchlight, cliff-tops, seas
where he would dive for pearls. My lover's words
were shooting stars which fell to earth as kisses
on these lips; my body now a softer rhyme
to his, now echo, assonance; his touch
a verb dancing in the centre of a noun.
Some nights I dreamed he'd written me, the bed
a page beneath his writer's hands. Romance
and drama played by touch, by scent, by taste.
In the other bed, the best, our guests dozed on,
dribbling their prose. My living laughing love –
I hold him in the casket of my widow's head
as he held me upon that next best bed.

PAUL LAURENCE DUNBAR

Douglass

Ah, Douglass, we have fall'n on evil days,
    Such days as thou, not even thou didst know,
    When thee, the eyes of that harsh long ago
Saw, salient, at the cross of devious ways,
And all the country heard thee with amaze.
    Not ended then, the passionate ebb and flow,
    The awful tide that battled to and fro;
We ride amid a tempest of dispraise.

Now, when the waves of swift dissension swarm,
    And Honor, the strong pilot, lieth stark,
Oh, for thy voice high-sounding o'er the storm,
    For thy strong arm to guide the shivering bark,
The blast-defying power of thy form,
    To give us comfort through the lonely dark.

ROBERT FROST

The Silken Tent

She is as in a field a silken tent
At midday when the sunny summer breeze
Has dried the dew and all its ropes relent,
So that in guys it gently sways at ease,
And its supporting central cedar pole,
That is its pinnacle to heavenward
And signifies the sureness of the soul,
Seems to owe naught to any single cord,
But strictly held by none, is loosely bound
By countless silken ties of love and thought
To everything on earth the compass round,
And only by one's going slightly taut
In the capriciousness of summer air
Is of the slightest bondage made aware.

Sonnet to George the Fourth

On the Repeal of Lord Edward Fitzgerald's Forfeiture

To be the father of the fatherless,
  To stretch the hand from the throne's height, and raise
  His offspring, who expired in other days
To make thy sire's sway by a kingdom less,—
This is to be a monarch, and repress
  Envy into unutterable praise.
  Dismiss thy guard, and trust thee to such traits,
For who would lift a hand, except to bless?
  Were it not easy, sir, and is't not sweet
  To make thyself beloved? and to be
Omnipotent by mercy's means? for thus
  Thy sovereignty would grow but more complete:
A despot thou, and yet thy people free,
  And by the heart, not hand, enslaving us.

THOMAS GRAY
On the Death of Richard West

In vain to me the smiling mornings shine,
And reddening Phoebus lifts his golden fire:
The birds in vain their amorous descant join,
Or cheerful fields resume their green attire:
These ears, alas! for other notes repine,
A different object do these eyes require.
My lonely anguish melts no heart but mine;
And in my breast the imperfect joys expire.
Yet morning smiles the busy race to cheer,
And new-born pleasure brings to happier men:
The fields to all their wonted tribute bear;
To warm their little loves the birds complain.
I fruitless mourn to him that cannot hear,
And weep the more because I weep in vain.

from *Cælica*

38

Cælica, I overnight was finely used,
Lodged in the midst of paradise, your heart;
Kind thoughts had charge I might not be refused,
Of every fruit and flower I had part.

But curious knowledge, blown with busy flame,
The sweetest fruits had in down shadows hidden,
And for it found mine eyes had seen the same,
I from my paradise was straight forbidden.

Where that cur, rumour, runs in every place,
Barking with care, begotten out of fear;
And glassy honour, tender of disgrace,
Stand seraphim to see I come not there;
    While that fine soil which all these joys did yield,
    By broken fence is proved a common field.

THOM GUNN

Lerici

Shelley was drowned near here. Arms at his side
He fell submissive through the waves, and he
Was but a minor conquest of the sea:
The darkness that he met was nurse not bride.

Others make gestures with arms open wide,
Compressing in the minute before death
What great expense of muscle and of breath
They would have made if they had never died.

Byron was worth the sea's pursuit. His touch
Was masterful to water, audience
To which he could react until an end.
Strong swimmers, fishermen, explorers: such
Dignify death by thriftless violence—
Squandering with so little left to spend.

IVOR GURNEY

September 1922

Fierce indignation is best understood by those
Who have time or no fear, or a hope in its real good.
One loses it with a filed soul or in sentimental mood.
Anger is gone with sunset, or flows as flows
The water in easy mill-runs; the earth that ploughs
Forgets protestation in its turning, the rood
Prepares, considers, fulfils; and the poppy's blood
Makes old the old changing of the headland's brows.

But the toad under the harrow toadiness
Is known to forget, and even the butterfly
Has doubts of wisdom when that clanking thing goes by
And's not distressed. A twisted thing keeps still –
That thing easier twisted than a grocer's bill –
And no history of November keeps the guy.

MARILYN HACKER
On Marriage

Epithalamion? Not too long back
I was being ironic about 'wives'.
It's very well to say, creation thrives
on contradiction, but that's a fast track
shifted precipitately into. Tacky,
some might say, and look mildly appalled. On
the whole, it's one I'm likely to be called on.
Explain yourself or face the music, Hack.
No law books frame terms of this covenant.
It's choice that's asymptotic to a goal,
which means that we must choose, and choose, and choose
momently, daily. This moment my whole
trajectory's toward you, and it's not losing
momentum. Call it anything we want.

KIMIKO HAHN

Reckless Sonnet No. 8

My father, as a boy in Milwaukee, thought
the cicada's cry was the whir from a live wire—
not from muscles on the sides of an insect
vibrating against an outer membrane. Strange though
that, because they have no ears, no one knows why
the males cry so doggedly into the gray air.
Not strange that the young live underground sucking sap from tree roots
for seventeen years. A long, charmed childhood
not unlike one in a Great Lake town where at dusk
you'd pack up swimsuit, shake sand off your towel
and head back to the lights in the two-family houses
lining the streets. Where the family sat around the radio.
And the parents argued over their son and daughter
until each left for good. To cry in the air.

THOMAS HARDY

Hap

If but some vengeful god would call to me
From up the sky, and laugh: 'Thou suffering thing,
Know that thy sorrow is my ecstasy,
That thy love's loss is my hate's profiting!'

Then would I bear it, clench myself, and die,
Steeled by the sense of ire unmerited;
Half-eased in that a Powerfuller than I
Had willed and meted me the tears I shed.

But not so. How arrives it joy lies slain,
And why unblooms the best hope ever sown?
—Crass Casualty obstructs the sun and rain,
And dicing Time for gladness casts a moan . . .
These purblind Doomsters had as readily strown
Blisses about my pilgrimage as pain.

TONY HARRISON

Long Distance II

Though my mother was already two years dead
Dad kept her slippers warming by the gas,
put hot water bottles her side of the bed
and still went to renew her transport pass.

You couldn't just drop in. You had to phone.
He'd put you off an hour to give him time
to clear away her things and look alone
as though his still raw love were such a crime.

He couldn't risk my blight of disbelief
though sure that very soon he'd hear her key
scrape in the rusted lock and end his grief.
He knew she'd just popped out to get the tea.

I believe life ends with death, and that is all.
You haven't both gone shopping; just the same,
in my new black leather phone book there's your name
and the disconnected number I still call.

GWEN HARWOOD

In the Bistro

A says 'You're right. He's brilliant but not sound.
This place has the true European fug.'
'Authentic.' B inhales it like a drug.
Tomorrow they will vote, and X be found
wanting. 'We know his kind, my boy. Once bitten . . .
The others will be easy to convince.
Let's try Caucasian whatsit.' (Curried mince.)
It must be twenty years since A has written
a useful word. B begs him to relate
old victories in academic wrangling.
He dreams of his promotion while A pours
a wine not too assertive. His hands wait
lax at his chest. One thinks of the small dangling
forelegs of the flesh-eating dinosaurs.

ROBERT HAYDEN

Those Winter Sundays

Sundays too my father got up early
and put his clothes on in the blueblack cold,
then with cracked hands that ached
from labor in the weekday weather made
banked fires blaze. No one ever thanked him.

I'd wake and hear the cold splintering, breaking.
When the rooms were warm, he'd call,
and slowly I would rise and dress,
fearing the chronic angers of that house,

Speaking indifferently to him,
who had driven out the cold
and polished my good shoes as well.
What did I know, what did I know
of love's austere and lonely offices?

TERRANCE HAYES

American Sonnet for My Past and Future Assassin

I lock you in an American sonnet that is part prison,
Part panic closet, a little room in a house set aflame.
I lock you in a form that is part music box, part meat
Grinder to separate the song of the bird from the bone.
I lock your persona in a dream-inducing sleeper hold
While your better selves watch from the bleachers.
I make you both gym & crow here. As the crow
You undergo a beautiful catharsis trapped one night
In the shadows of the gym. As the gym, the feel of crow-
Shit dropping to your floors is not unlike the stars
Falling from the pep rally posters on your walls.
I make you a box of darkness with a bird in its heart.
Voltas of acoustics, instinct & metaphor. It is not enough
To love you. It is not enough to want you destroyed.

Requiem for the Croppies

The pockets of our greatcoats full of barley –
No kitchens on the run, no striking camp –
We moved quick and sudden in our own country.
The priest lay behind ditches with the tramp.
A people, hardly marching – on the hike –
We found new tactics happening each day:
We'd cut through reins and rider with the pike
And stampede cattle into infantry,
Then retreat through hedges where cavalry must be thrown.
Until, on Vinegar Hill, the fatal conclave.
Terraced thousands died, shaking scythes at cannon.
The hillside blushed, soaked in our broken wave.
They buried us without shroud or coffin
And in August the barley grew up out of the grave.

GEORGE HERBERT

Redemption

Having been tenant long to a rich lord,
    Not thriving, I resolvèd to be bold
    And make a suit unto him, to afford
A new small-rented lease, and cancel th'old.
In heaven at his manor I him sought:
    They told me there that he was lately gone
    About some land, which he had dearly bought
Long since on earth, to take possession.
I straight returned, and knowing his great birth
    Sought him accordingly in great resorts,
    In cities, theatres, gardens, parks and courts.
At length I heard a ragged noise and mirth
    Of thieves and murderers: there I him espied,
    Who straight 'Your suit is granted' said, and died.

Delight in Disorder

A sweet disorder in the dress
Kindles in clothes a wantonness:
A lawn about the shoulders thrown
Into a fine distraction:
An erring lace which here and there
Enthralls the crimson stomacher:
A cuff neglectful, and thereby
Ribands to flow confusedly:
A winning wave (deserving note)
In the tempestuous petticoat:
A careless shoestring, in whose tie
I see a wild civility:
Do more bewitch me, than when art
Is too precise in every part.

GERARD MANLEY HOPKINS

The Windhover

To Christ Our Lord

I caught this morning morning's mínion, king-
    dom of daylight's dauphin, dapple-dáwn-drawn Falcon, in his riding
    Of the rólling level úndernéath him steady aír, and stríding
High there, how he rung upon the rein of a wimpling wing
In his écstasy! then off, off forth on swing,
    As a skate's heel sweeps smooth on a bow-bend: the hurl and gliding
    Rebuffed the bíg wínd. My heart in hiding
Stírred for a bird,—the achieve of, the mástery of the thing!

Brute beauty and valour and act, oh, air, pride, plúme, here
    Buckle! AND the fire that breaks from thee then, a billion
Tímes told lovelier, more dangerous, O my chevalier!

    No wónder of it: shéer plód makes plough down sillion
Shíne, and blue-bleak embers, ah my dear,
    Fall, gáll themsélves, and gásh góld-vermílion.

I never saw you, madam, lay apart

I never saw you, madam, lay apart
   Your cornet black, in cold nor yet in heat,
   Sith first ye knew of my desire so great,
Which other fancies chased clean from my heart.
Whiles to my self I did the thought reserve,
   That so unware did wound my woeful breast,
   Pity I saw within your heart did rest.
But since ye knew I did you love and serve,
Your golden tress was clad alway in black,
   Your smiling looks were hid thus evermore,
   All that withdrawn that I did crave so sore.
So doth this cornet govern me, alack!
   In summer's sun, in winter breath of frost,
   Of your fair eyes whereby the light is lost.

Iterating Sonnet

Written during the talk of a war between
England and the United States

War between England and the United States!
    Impossible! Pshaw! Stuff!—'United States!'
    Why, they themselves are the United States:
    London and Boston are United States:
New York and Liverpool United States:
    Cotton and spinning very United States:
    Progress and liberty, United States:
    Their names, fames, books, bloods, all United States.
But 'bloods are up' in the United States?
    Well;—would'st have 'low' bloods in the United States?
    No: high bloods—high—in both United States:
So high, that, seeing their United States,
    They scorn to stoop from such United States
    Solely to please poor *dis*-United States.

TYEHIMBA JESS

from *Sonnet Crown for Blind Tom*

Blind Tom plays for Confederate Troops, 1863

The slave's hands dance free, unfettered, flying
across ivory, feet stomping toward
a crescendo that fills the forest pine,
reminding the Rebs what they're fighting for –
black, captive labor. Tom, slick with sweat, shows
a new trick: Back turned to his piano,
he leans like a runner about to throw
himself to freedom through forest bramble –
until he spreads his hands behind him. He
hitches fingertips to keys, hauls Dixie
slowly out of the battered upright's teeth
like a worksong dragged across cotton fields,
like a plow, weighted and dirty, ringing
with a slaver's song at master's bidding.

A Sonnet to the Noble Lady,
the Lady Mary Wroth

I that have been a lover, and could shew it,
   Though not in these, in rithmes not wholly dumb,
   Since I exscribe your sonnets, am become
   A better lover, and much better poet.
Nor is my Muse or I ashamed to owe it
   To those true numerous graces; whereof some
   But charm the senses, others overcome
   Both brains and hearts; and mine now best do know it:
For in your verse all Cupid's armoury,
   His flames, his shafts, his quiver, and his bow,
   His very eyes are yours to overthrow.
But then his mother's sweets you so apply,
   Her joys, her smiles, her loves, as readers take
   For Venus' ceston every line you make.

Epic

I have lived in important places, times
When great events were decided, who owned
That half a rood of rock, a no-man's land
Surrounded by our pitchfork-armed claims.
I heard the Duffys shouting 'Damn your soul'
And old McCabe stripped to the waist, seen
Step the plot defying blue cast-steel—
'Here is the march along these iron stones'
That was the year of the Munich bother. Which
Was more important? I inclined
To lose my faith in Ballyrush and Gortin
Till Homer's ghost came whispering to my mind
He said: I made the Iliad from such
A local row. Gods make their own importance.

JOHN KEATS

If by dull rhymes our English must be chain'd

If by dull rhymes our English must be chain'd,
   And, like Andromeda, the sonnet sweet
Fetter'd, in spite of pained loveliness;
Let us find out, if we must be constrain'd,
   Sandals more interwoven and complete
To fit the naked foot of Poesy;
Let us inspect the lyre, and weigh the stress
Of every chord, and see what may be gain'd
   By ear industrious, and attention meet;
Misers of sound and syllable, no less
Than Midas of his coinage, let us be
   Jealous of dead leaves in the bay wreath crown;
So, if we may not let the muse be free,
   She will be bound with garlands of her own.

To Robert Browning

There is delight in singing, tho' none hear
Beside the singer; and there is delight
In praising, tho' the praiser sit alone
And see the prais'd far off him, far above.
Shakspeare is not our poet, but the world's,
Therefore on him no speech! and brief for thee,
Browning! Since Chaucer was alive and hale,
No man hath walkt along our roads with step
So active, so inquiring eye, or tongue
So varied in discourse. But warmer climes
Give brighter plumage, stronger wing: the breeze
Of Alpine highths thou playest with, borne on
Beyond Sorrento and Amalfi, where
The Siren waits thee, singing song for song.

Love, we must part now: do not let it be

Love, we must part now: do not let it be
Calamitous and bitter. In the past
There has been too much moonlight and self-pity:
Let us have done with it: for now at last
Never has sun more boldly paced the sky,
Never were hearts more eager to be free,
To kick down worlds, lash forests; you and I
No longer hold them; we are husks, that see
The grain going forward to a different use.

There is regret. Always, there is regret.
But it is better that our lives unloose,
As two tall ships, wind-mastered, wet with light,
Break from an estuary with their courses set,
And waving part, and waving drop from sight.

EMMA LAZARUS

The New Colossus

Not like the brazen giant of Greek fame,
With conquering limbs astride from land to land;
Here at our sea-washed, sunset gates shall stand
A mighty woman with a torch, whose flame
Is the imprisoned lightning, and her name
Mother of Exiles. From her beacon-hand
Glows world-wide welcome; her mild eyes command
The air-bridged harbor that twin cities frame.
'Keep, ancient lands, your storied pomp!' cries she
With silent lips. 'Give me your tired, your poor,
Your huddled masses yearning to breathe free,
The wretched refuse of your teeming shore.
Send these, the homeless, tempest-tost to me,
I lift my lamp beside the golden door!'

BRAD LEITHAUSER

Post-Coitum Tristesse: A Sonnet

Why
do
you
sigh,
roar,
fall,
all
for
some
hum-
drum
come
—mm?
Hm . . .

ANNE LOCKE

Sonnet

Have mercy, God, for thy great mercy's sake.
O God: my God, unto my shame I say,
Being fled from thee, so as I dread to take
Thy name in wretched mouth, and fear to pray
Or ask the mercy that I have abused.
But, God of mercy, let me come to thee:
Not for justice, that justly am accused:
Which self word Justice so amazeth me,
That scarce I dare thy mercy sound again.
But mercy, Lord, yet suffer me to crave.
Mercy is thine: Let me not cry in vain,
Thy great mercy for my great fault to have.
Have mercy, God, pity my penitence
With greater mercy than my great offence.

MICHAEL LONGLEY
Florence Nightingale

Through your pocket glass you have let disease expand
To remote continents of pain where you go far
With rustling cuff and starched apron, a soft hand:
Beneath the bandage maggots are stitching the scar.

For many of the men who lie there it is late
And you allow them at the edge of consciousness
The halo of your lamp, a brothel's fanlight
Or a nightlight carried in by nanny and nurse.

You know that even with officers and clergy
Moustachioed lips will purse into fundaments
And under sedation all the bad words emerge
To be rinsed in your head like the smell of wounds,

Death's vegetable sweetness at both rind and core –
Name a weed and you find it growing everywhere.

Chaucer

An old man in a lodge within a park;
  The chamber walls depicted all around
  With portraitures of huntsman, hawk, and hound,
  And the hurt deer. He listeneth to the lark,
Whose song comes with the sunshine through the dark
  Of painted glass in leaden lattice bound;
  He listeneth and he laugheth at the sound,
  Then writeth in a book like any clerk.
He is the poet of the dawn, who wrote
  The Canterbury Tales, and his old age
  Made beautiful with song; and as I read
I hear the crowing cock, I hear the note
  Of lark and linnet, and from every page
  Rise odors of ploughed field or flowery mead.

'To Speak of Woe That Is in Marriage'

*It is the future generation that presses into being by means of
these exuberant feelings and supersensible soap bubbles of ours.*

SCHOPENHAUER

'The hot night makes us keep our bedroom windows open.
Our magnolia blossoms. Life begins to happen.
My hopped up husband drops his home disputes,
and hits the streets to cruise for prostitutes,
free-lancing out along the razor's edge.
This screwball might kill his wife, then take the pledge.
Oh the monotonous meanness of his lust . . .
It's the injustice . . . he is so unjust—
whiskey-blind, swaggering home at five.
My only thought is how to keep alive.
What makes him tick? Each night now I tie
ten dollars and his car key to my thigh . . .
Gored by the climacteric of his want,
he stalls above me like an elephant.'

SHANE McCRAE

Jim Limber the Adopted Mulatto Son of Jefferson Davis Was Another Child First

They put me in a dead boy's clothes dead Joseph

Except he wasn't dead at first they put

Me in his clothes dead Joseph's   after Joseph

Died and I used to call him Joe   they put

Me in Joe's clothes at first before he died

Joe wasn't five yet when I met him   I

Was seven   I was seven when he died

Still but a whole year bigger then but I

Wore his clothes still and the whole year I lived with

Momma Varina   and with daddy Jeff

I never lived so good as when I lived with

Them and especially it was daddy Jeff

Who kept me fed and wearing those nice clothes

Until they fit as tight as bandages

CLAUDE McKAY

If We Must Die

If we must die, let it not be like hogs
Hunted and penned in an inglorious spot,
While round us bark the mad and hungry dogs,
Making their mock at our accurséd lot.
If we must die, O let us nobly die,
So that our precious blood may not be shed
In vain; then even the monsters we defy
Shall be constrained to honor us though dead!
O kinsmen! we must meet the common foe!
Though far outnumbered let us show us brave,
And for their thousand blows deal one deathblow!
What though before us lies the open grave?
Like men we'll face the murderous, cowardly pack,
Pressed to the wall, dying, but fighting back!

Sunday Morning

Down the road someone is practising scales,
The notes like little fishes vanish with a wink of tails,
Man's heart expands to tinker with his car
For this is Sunday morning, Fate's great bazaar;
Regard these means as ends, concentrate on this Now,
And you may grow to music or drive beyond Hindhead anyhow,
Take corners on two wheels until you go so fast
That you can clutch a fringe or two of the windy past,
That you can abstract this day and make it to the week of time
A small eternity, a sonnet self-contained in rhyme.

But listen, up the road, something gulps, the church spire
Opens its eight bells out, skulls' mouths which will not tire
To tell how there is no music or movement which secures
Escape from the weekday time. Which deadens and endures.

GEORGE MEREDITH
Lucifer in Starlight

On a starred night Prince Lucifer uprose.
Tired of his dark dominion swung the fiend
Above the rolling ball in cloud part screened,
Where sinners hugged their spectre of repose.
Poor prey to his hot fit of pride were those.
And now upon his western wing he leaned,
Now his huge bulk o'er Afric's sands careened,
Now the black planet shadowed Arctic snows.
Soaring through wider zones that pricked his scars
With memory of the old revolt from Awe,
He reached a middle height, and at the stars,
Which are the brain of heaven, he looked, and sank.
Around the ancient track marched, rank on rank,
The army of unalterable law.

CHARLOTTE MEW

Not for That City

Not for that city of the level sun,
      Its golden streets and glittering gates ablaze –
      The shadeless, sleepless city of white days,
White nights, or nights and days that are as one –
We weary, when all is said, all thought, all done,
      We strain our eyes beyond this dusk to see
      What, from the threshold of eternity
We shall step into. No, I think we shun
The splendour of that everlasting glare,
  The clamour of that never-ending song.
  And if for anything we greatly long,
It is for some remote and quiet stair
      Which winds to silence and a space for sleep
      Too sound for waking and for dreams too deep.

EDNA ST VINCENT MILLAY

I will put Chaos into fourteen lines

I will put Chaos into fourteen lines
And keep him there; and let him thence escape
If he be lucky; let him twist, and ape
Flood, fire, and demon—his adroit designs
Will strain to nothing in the strict confines
Of this sweet Order, where, in pious rape,
I hold his essence and amorphous shape,
Till he with Order mingles and combines.
Past are the hours, the years, of our duress,
His arrogance, our awful servitude:
I have him. He is nothing more nor less
Than something simple not yet understood;
I shall not even force him to confess;
Or answer. I will only make him good.

JOHN MILTON

When I consider how my light is spent

When I consider how my light is spent,
    Ere half my days, in this dark world and wide,
    And that one talent which is death to hide,
    Lodg'd with me useless, though my soul more bent
To serve therewith my Maker, and present
    My true account, lest he returning chide;
    'Doth God exact day-labour, light denied,'
    I fondly ask; but patience, to prevent
That murmur, soon replies, 'God doth not need
    Either man's work or his own gifts; who best
    Bear his mild yoke, they serve him best; his state
Is kingly. Thousands at his bidding speed
    And post o'er land and ocean without rest:
    They also serve who only stand and wait.'

HOPE MIRRLEES
The Glass Tánagra

I dreamt that I had wandered far away
To landscapes that were alien and rococo,
And knew that I was living long ago
For Wedgwood had just started 'throwing clay'.
But in my dream the fashion of the day
Were tánagras that Nereids might blow
From moonlight, foam, and sunsets at Murano,
And one small chef-d'oeuvre filled me with dismay.
And as I watched what seemed my tears roll down
The spotless uncreased drapery of glass,
Making it shine like dew on summer grass,
In sudden rage I smashed it with a stone.
And then I heard the gentle Petrarch moan,
'The broken thing is her own heart, alas!'

Milton

Milton, his face set fair for Paradise,
And knowing that he and Paradise were lost
In separate desolation, bravely crossed
Into his second night and paid his price.
There towards the end he to the dark tower came
Set square in the gate, a mass of blackened stone
Crowned with vermilion fiends like streamers blown
From a great funnel filled with roaring flame.

Shut in his darkness, these he could not see,
But heard the steely clamour known too well
On Saturday nights in every street in Hell.
Where, past the devilish din, could Paradise be?
A footstep more, and his unblinded eyes
Saw far and near the fields of Paradise.

LES MURRAY
The Mitchells

I am seeing this: two men are sitting on a pole
they have dug a hole for and will, after dinner, raise
I think for wires. Water boils in a prune tin.
Bees hum their shift in unthinning mists of white

bursaria blossom, under the noon of wattles.
The men eat big meat sandwiches out of a styrofoam
box with a handle. One is overheard saying:
drought that year. Yes. Like trying to farm the road.

The first man, if asked, would say *I'm one of the Mitchells.*
The other would gaze for a while, dried leaves in his palm,
and looking up, with pain and subtle amusement,

say *I'm one of the Mitchells.* Of the pair, one has been rich
but never stopped wearing his oil-stained felt hat. Nearly everything
they say is ritual. Sometimes the scene is an avenue.

MARILYN NELSON

from *A Wreath for Emmett Till*

IV

Emmett Till's name still catches in my throat,
like syllables waylaid in a stutterer's mouth.
A fourteen-year-old stutterer, in the South
to visit relatives and to be taught
the family's ways. His mother had finally bought
that White Sox cap; she'd made him swear an oath
to be careful around white folks. She's told him the truth
of many a Mississippi anecdote:
Some white folks have blind souls. In his suitcase
she'd packed dungarees, T-shirts, underwear,
and comic books. She'd given him a note
for the conductor, waved to his chubby face,
wondered if he'd remember to brush his hair.
Her only child. A body left to bloat.

EILÉAN NÍ CHUILLEANÁIN
Swineherd

When all this is over, said the swineherd,
I mean to retire, where
nobody will have heard about my special skills
and conversation is mainly about the weather.

I intend to learn how to make coffee, as least as well
as the Portuguese lay-sister in the kitchen
and polish the brass fenders every day.
I want to lie awake at night
listening to cream crawling to the top of the jug
and the water lying soft in the cistern.

I want to see an orchard where the trees grow in straight lines
and the yellow fox finds shelter between the navy-blue trunks,
where it gets dark early in summer
and the apple-blossom is allowed to wither on the bough.

ALICE OSWALD

Sea Sonnet

The sea is made of ponds – a cairn of rain.
It has an island flirting up and down
like a blue hat. A boat goes in between.

Is made of rills and springs – each waternode
a tiny subjectivity, the tide
coordinates their ends, the sea is made.

The sea crosses sea, the sea has hooves;
the powers of rivers and the weir's curves
are moving in the wind-bent acts of waves.

And then the softer waters of the wells
and soakaways – hypostases of holes,
which swallow up and sink for seven miles;

and then the boat arriving on the island
and nothing but the sea-like sea beyond.

WILFRED OWEN
Anthem for Doomed Youth

What passing-bells for these who die as cattle?
   Only the monstrous anger of the guns.
   Only the stuttering rifles' rapid rattle
Can patter out their hasty orisons.
No mockeries now for them; no prayers nor bells,
   Nor any voice of mourning save the choirs,—
The shrill, demented choirs of wailing shells;
   And bugles calling for them from sad shires.

What candles may be held to speed them all?
   Not in the hands of boys, but in their eyes
Shall shine the holy glimmers of goodbyes.
   The pallor of girls' brows shall be their pall;
Their flowers the tenderness of patient minds,
And each slow dusk a drawing-down of blinds.

DON PATERSON

Wave

For months I'd moved across the open water
like a wheel under its skin, a frictionless
and by then almost wholly abstract matter
with nothing in my head beyond the bliss
of my own breaking, how the long foreshore
would hear my full confession, and I'd drain
into the shale till I was filtered pure.
There was no way to tell on that bare plain
but I felt my power run down with the miles
and by the time I saw the scattered sails,
the painted front and children on the pier
I was nothing but a fold in her blue gown
and knew I was already in the clear.
I hit the beach and swept away the town.

CARL PHILLIPS

Invasive Species

Switchgrass beachgrass trespass
little song. Little song years remastering truth
now begins its own truth little song

deep in the night. Not a wreath more a
crown little song worn shyly. Past
regret little song no weep remembering

nor long for. Little song done with tears
though nowhere anyone not somehow hand
in hand little song still lonely undaunted un-
persuaded. Persuasion a meadow once

violence the field
seeding itself with its own flower. For fist
little song. Up from the dragged lake of the singer's throat
little song severed fist in the light turning. It shines in the light.

SYLVIA PLATH

Mayflower

Throughout black winter the red haws withstood
Assault of snow-flawed winds from the dour skies
And, bright as blood-drops, proved no brave branch dies
If root's firm-fixed and resolution good.
Now, as green sap ascends the steepled wood,
Each hedge with such white bloom astounds our eyes
As sprang from Joseph's rod, and testifies
How best beauty's born of hardihood.

So when staunch island stock chose forfeiture
Of the homeland hearth to plough their pilgrim way
Across Atlantic furrows, dark, unsure—
Remembering the white, triumphant spray
On hawthorn boughs, with goodwill to endure
They named their ship after the flower of May.

EDGAR ALLAN POE

Sonnet—To Science

Science! true daughter of Old Time thou art!
  Who alterest all things with thy peering eyes.
Why preyest thou thus upon the poet's heart,
  Vulture, whose wings are dull realities?
How should he love thee? or how deem thee wise,
  Who wouldst not leave him in his wandering
To seek for treasure in the jewelled skies,
  Albeit he soared with an undaunted wing?
Hast thou not dragged Diana from her car,
  And driven the Hamadryad from the wood
To seek a shelter in some happier star?
  Hast thou not torn the Naiad from her flood,
The Elfin from the green grass, and from me
The summer dream beneath the tamarind tree?

MARIE PONSOT

One Is One

Heart, you bully, you punk, I'm wrecked, I'm shocked
stiff. You? you still try to rule the world—though
I've got you: identified, starving, locked
in a cage you will not leave alive, no
matter how you hate it, pound its walls,
& thrill its corridors with messages.

Brute. Spy. I trusted you. Now you reel & brawl
in your cell but I'm deaf to your rages,
your greed to go solo, your eloquent
threats of worse things you (knowing me) could do.
You scare me, bragging you're a double agent

since jailers are prisoners' prisoners too.
Think! Reform! Make us one. Join the rest of us,
and joy may come, and make its test of us.

SIR WALTER RALEIGH
Sir Walter Raleigh to his son

Three things there be that prosper up apace
And flourish, whilst they grow asunder far,
But on a day they meet all in one place
And when they meet they one another mar,
And they be these: the wood, the weed, the wag.
The wood is that which makes the gallow-tree,
The weed is that which strings the hangman's bag,
The wag, my pretty knave, betokeneth thee.
Mark well, dear boy, whilst these assemble not,
Green springs the tree, hemp grows, the wag is wild,
But when they meet it makes the timber rot,
It frets the halter and it chokes the child.
    Then bless thee, and beware, and let us pray
    We part not with thee at this meeting day.

RAINER MARIA RILKE

The Unicorn

This, then, is the beast that has never actually been:
not having seen one, they prized in any case
its perfect poise, its throat, the straightforward gaze
it gave them back—so straightforward, so serene.

Since it had never been, it was all the more
unsullied. And they allowed it such latitude
that, in a clearing in the wood,
it raised its head as if its essence shrugged off mere

existence. They brought it on, not with oats or corn,
but with the chance, however slight,
that it might come into its own. This gave it such strength

that from its brow there sprang a horn. A single horn.
Only when it met a maiden's white with white
would it be bodied out in her, in her mirror's full length.

translated by Paul Muldoon

ED ROBERSON

Poems, Sunrises, and Precedents

On sonnet form

times even in the grip of trouble
get no less a sunrise than sun is capable
the capable beauty all we have
to expect—   to ask more from some incompetent   laughs

at the proposition   we have trumped all that
from such horses as
we have   pulling our wagon through the dust
which we   ourselves yoked to the lead   that trust—

people of the voice though we were.
people who cannot figure
what it is we want to say for us—

if all we have is the form to stuff
as the end   then any poem of the times comes up
capable as shining.   shining or not.   enveloped.

Fleming Helphenstine

At first I thought there was a superfine
Persuasion in his face; but the free glow
That filled it when he stopped and cried, 'Hollo!'
Shone joyously, and so I let it shine.
He said his name was Fleming Helphenstine,
But be that as it may;—I only know
He talked of this and that and So-and-So,
And laughed and chaffed like any friend of mine.

But soon, with a queer, quick frown, he looked at me,
And I looked hard at him; and there we gazed
In a strained way that made us cringe and wince:
Then, with a wordless clogged apology
That sounded half confused and half amazed,
He dodged,—and I have never seen him since.

THEODORE ROETHKE
The Favorite

A knave who scampered through the needle's eye,
He never trembled at a veiled remark.
His oyster world was easily come by;
There were no nights of sleeping in the park.

Fearless and bold, he did his fellows in,
Only to gain fresh triumphs and applause.
His insolence could wear no patience thin.
He lived beyond the touch of mortal laws.

O he was Fortune's child, a favorite son
Upon whom every gift and thrill were showered,
And yet his happiness was not complete;
Slowly his matchless disposition soured
Until he cried at enemies undone
And longed to feel the impact of defeat.

CHRISTINA ROSSETTI
from *Monna Innominata*

Many in aftertimes will say of you
'He loved her'—while of me what will they say?
   Not that I loved you more than just in play,
For fashion's sake as idle women do.
Even let them prate; who know not what we knew
   Of love and parting in exceeding pain,
   Of parting hopeless here to meet again,
Hopeless on earth, and heaven is out of view.
But by my heart of love laid bare to you,
   My love that you can make not void nor vain,
Love that foregoes you but to claim anew
   Beyond this passage of the gate of death,
I charge you at the Judgment make it plain
   My love of you was life and not a breath.

DANTE GABRIEL ROSSETTI
Willowwood

I

I sat with Love upon a woodside well,
    Leaning across the water, I and he;
    Nor ever did he speak nor looked at me,
But touched his lute wherein was audible
The certain secret thing he had to tell:
    Only our mirrored eyes met silently
    In the low wave; and that sound came to be
The passionate voice I knew; and my tears fell.

And at their fall, his eyes beneath grew hers;
And with his foot and with his wing-feathers
    He swept the spring that watered my heart's drouth.
Then the dark ripples spread to waving hair,
And as I stooped, her own lips rising there
    Bubbled with brimming kisses at my mouth.

And now Love sang: but his was such a song,
    So meshed with half-remembrance hard to free,
    As souls disused in death's sterility
May sing when the new birthday tarries long.
And I was made aware of a dumb throng
    That stood aloof, one form by every tree,
    All mournful forms, for each was I or she,
The shades of those our days that had no tongue.

They looked on us, and knew us and were known;
    While fast together, alive from the abyss,
    Clung the soul-wrung implacable close kiss;
And pity of self through all made broken moan
Which said, 'For once, for once, for once alone!'
    And still Love sang, and what he sang was this:—

'O ye, all ye that walk in Willowwood,
    That walk with hollow faces burning white;
What fathom-depth of soul-struck widowhood,
    What long, what longer hours, one lifelong night,
Ere ye again, who so in vain have wooed
    Your last hope lost, who so in vain invite
Your lips to that their unforgotten food,
    Ere ye, ere ye again shall see the light!

Alas! the bitter banks in Willowwood,
    With tear-spurge wan, with blood-wort burning red:
Alas! if ever such a pillow could
    Steep deep the soul in sleep till she were dead,—
Better all life forget her than this thing,
That Willowwood should hold her wandering!'

So sang he: and as meeting rose and rose
　　Together cling through the wind's wellaway,
　　Nor change at once, yet near the end of day
The leaves drop loosened where the heart-stain glows,—
So when the song died did the kiss unclose;
　　And her face fell back drowned, and was as grey
　　As its grey eyes; and if it ever may
Meet mine again I know not if Love knows.

Only I know that I leaned low and drank
A long draught from the water where she sank,
　　Her breath and all her tears and all her soul:
And as I leaned, I know I felt Love's face
Pressed on my neck with moan of pity and grace,
　　Till both our heads were in his aureole.

SIEGFRIED SASSOON

Trench Duty

Shaken from sleep, and numbed and scarce awake,
Out in the trench with three hours' watch to take,
I blunder through the splashing mirk; and then
Hear the gruff muttering voices of the men
Crouching in cabins candle-chinked with light.
Hark! There's the big bombardment on our right
Rumbling and bumping; and the dark's a glare
Of flickering horror in the sectors where
We raid the Bosche; men waiting, stiff and chilled,
Or crawling on their bellies through the wire.
'What? Stretcher-bearers wanted? Some one killed?'
Five minutes ago I heard a sniper fire:
Why did he do it? . . . Starlight overhead—
Blank stars. I'm wide-awake; and some chap's dead.

ANNA SEWARD

To the Poppy

While summer roses all their glory yield
    To crown the votary of Love and Joy,
    Misfortune's victim hails, with many a sigh,
    Thee, scarlet poppy of the pathless field,
Gaudy, yet wild and lone; no leaf to shield
    Thy flaccid vest, that, as the gale blows high,
    Flaps, and alternate folds around thy head.—
    So stands in the long grass a love-crazed maid
Smiling aghast; while stream to every wind
    Her garish ribbons, smeared with dust and rain;
    But brain-sick visions cheat her tortured mind,
And bring false peace. Thus, lulling grief and pain,
    Kind dreams oblivious from thy juice proceed,
    Thou flimsy, showy, melancholy weed.

WILLIAM SHAKESPEARE

Sonnet 116

Let me not to the marriage of true minds
Admit impediments; love is not love
Which alters when it alteration finds
Or bends with the remover to remove.
O, no, it is an ever-fixèd mark
That looks on tempests and is never shaken;
It is the star to every wand'ring bark,
Whose worth's unknown, although his height be taken.
Love's not Time's fool, though rosy lips and cheeks
Within his bending sickle's compass come;
Love alters not with his brief hours and weeks,
But bears it out even to the edge of doom.
   If this be error, and upon me proved,
    I never writ, nor no man ever loved.

Ozymandias

I met a traveller from an antique land,
Who said—'Two vast and trunkless legs of stone
Stand in the desart . . . Near them, on the sand,
Half sunk a shattered visage lies, whose frown,
And wrinkled lip, and sneer of cold command,
Tell that its sculptor well those passions read
Which yet survive, stamped on these lifeless things,
The hand that mocked them, and the heart that fed;
And on the pedestal, these words appear:
My name is Ozymandias, King of Kings,
Look on my Works, ye Mighty, and despair!
Nothing beside remains. Round the decay
Of that colossal Wreck, boundless and bare
The lone and level sands stretch far away.'

SIR PHILIP SIDNEY
from *Astrophel and Stella*

31

With how sad steps, O Moon, thou climb'st the skies,
How silently, and with how wan a face,
What may it be, that even in heav'nly place
That busie archer his sharp arrows tries?
Sure, if that long with Love acquainted eyes
Can judge of Love, thou feel'st a Lover's case;
I read it in thy looks, thy languish'd grace
To me that feel the like, thy state descries.
Then ev'n of fellowship, O Moon, tell me
Is constant Love deem'd there but want of wit?
Are Beauties there as proud as here they be?
Do they above love to be lov'd, and yet
Those Lovers scorn whom that Love doth possess?
Do they call Virtue there ungratefulness?

CHARLOTTE SMITH

Composed during a Walk on the Downs, in November 1787

The dark and pillowy cloud; the sallow trees,
Seem o'er the ruins of the year to mourn;
And cold and hollow, the inconstant breeze
Sobs thro' the falling leaves and withered fern.
O'er the tall brow of yonder chalky bourn,
The evening-shades their gathered darkness fling,
While, by the lingering light, I scarce discern
The shrieking night-jar, sail on heavy wing.
Ah! yet a little—and propitious Spring
Crowned with fresh flowers, shall wake the woodland strain;
But no gay change revolving seasons bring,
To call forth pleasure from the soul of pain,
Bid syren Hope resume her long-lost part,
And chase the vulture Care—that feeds upon the heart.

PATRICIA SMITH

from *Motown Crown*

The Temps, all swerve and pivot, conjured schemes
that had us skipping school, made us forget
how mamas schooled us hard against the threat
of five-part harmony and sharkskin seams.
We spent our schooldays balanced on the beams
of moon we wished upon, the needled jetblack
45s that spun and hadn't yet
become the dizzy spinning of our dreams.
Sugar Pie, Honey Bun, oh you
loved our nappy hair and rusty knees.
Marvin Gaye slowed down while we gave chase
and then he was our smokin' fine taboo.
We hungered for the anguished screech of *Please*
inside our chests—relentless, booming bass.

ROBERT SOUTHEY

To a Goose

If thou didst feed on western plains of yore;
Or waddle wide with flat and flabby feet
Over some Cambrian mountain's plashy moor;
Or find in farmer's yard a safe retreat
From gypsy thieves, and foxes sly and fleet;
If thy grey quills, by lawyer guided, trace
Deeds big with ruin to some wretched race,
Or love-sick poet's sonnet, sad and sweet,
Wailing the rigour of his lady fair;
Or if, the drudge of housemaid's daily toil,
Cobwebs and dust thy pinions white besoil,
Departed Goose! I neither know nor care.
But this I know, that we pronounced thee fine,
Seasoned with sage and onions, and port wine.

EDMUND SPENSER

from *Amoretti*

75

One day I wrote her name upon the strand;
But came the waves, and washed it away:
Again, I wrote it with a second hand;
But came the tide, and made my pains his prey.
Vain man! said she, that dost in vain assay
A mortal thing so to immortalise;
For I myself shall like to this decay,
And eke my name be wiped out likewise.
Not so (quod I); let baser things devise
To die in dust, but you shall live by fame:
My verse your vertues rare shall eternise,
And in the heavens write your glorious name;
Where, when as death shall all the world subdue,
Our love shall live, and later life renew.

A Sequence of Sonnets
on the Death of Robert Browning

I

The clearest eyes in all the world they read
　　With sense more keen and spirit of sight more true
　　Than burns and thrills in sunrise, when the dew
Flames, and absorbs the glory round it shed,
As they the light of ages quick and dead,
　　Closed now, forsake us: yet the shaft that slew
　　Can slay not one of all the works we knew,
Nor death discrown that many-laurelled head.

The works of words whose life seems lightning wrought,
And moulded of unconquerable thought,
　　And quickened with imperishable flame,
Stand fast and shine and smile, assured that nought
　　May fade of all their myriad-moulded fame,
　　Nor England's memory clasp not Browning's name.

Death, what hast thou to do with one for whom
    Time is not lord, but servant? What least part
    Of all the fire that fed his living heart,
Of all the light more keen than sundawn's bloom
That lit and led his spirit, strong as doom
    And bright as hope, can aught thy breath may dart
    Quench? Nay, thou knowest he knew thee what thou art,
A shadow born of terror's barren womb,
That brings not forth save shadows. What art thou,
To dream, albeit thou breathe upon his brow,
    That power on him is given thee,—that thy breath
Can make him less than love acclaims him now,
    And hears all time sound back the word it saith?
    What part hast thou then in his glory, Death?

III

A graceless doom it seems that bids us grieve:
 Venice and winter, hand in deadly hand,
 Have slain the lover of her sunbright strand
And singer of a stormbright Christmas Eve.
A graceless guerdon we that loved receive
 For all our love, from that the dearest land
 Love worshipped ever. Blithe and soft and bland,
Too fair for storm to scathe or fire to cleave,
Shone on our dreams and memories evermore
The domes, the towers, the mountains and the shore
 That gird or guard thee, Venice: cold and black
Seems now the face we loved as he of yore.
 We have given thee love—no stint, no stay, no lack:
 What gift, what gift is this thou hast given us back?

IV

But he—to him, who knows what gift is thine,
    Death? Hardly may we think or hope, when we
    Pass likewise thither where to-night is he,
Beyond the irremeable outer seas that shine
And darken round such dreams as half divine
    Some sunlit harbour in that starless sea
    Where gleams no ship to windward or to lee,
To read with him the secret of thy shrine.

There too, as here, may song, delight, and love,
The nightingale, the sea-bird, and the dove,
    Fulfil with joy the splendour of the sky
Till all beneath wax bright as all above:
    But none of all that search the heavens, and try
    The sun, may match the sovereign eagle's eye.

v

Among the wondrous ways of men and time
    He went as one that ever found and sought
    And bore in hand the lamp-like spirit of thought
To illume with instance of its fire sublime
The dusk of many a cloudlike age and clime.
    No spirit in shape of light and darkness wrought,
    No faith, no fear, no dream, no rapture, nought
That blooms in wisdom, nought that burns in crime,
No virtue girt and armed and helmed with light,
No love more lovely than the snows are white,
    No serpent sleeping in some dead soul's tomb,
No song-bird singing from some live soul's height,
    But he might hear, interpret, or illume
    With sense invasive as the dawn of doom.

VI

What secret thing of splendour or of shade
    Surmised in all those wandering ways wherein
    Man, led of love and life and death and sin,
Strays, climbs, or cowers, allured, absorbed, afraid,
Might not the strong and sunlike sense invade
    Of that full soul that had for aim to win
    Light, silent over time's dark toil and din,
Life, at whose touch death fades as dead things fade?
O spirit of man, what mystery moves in thee
That he might know not of in spirit, and see
    The heart within the heart that seems to strive,
The life within the life that seems to be,
    And hear, through all thy storms that whirl and drive,
    The living sound of all men's souls alive?

He held no dream worth waking: so he said,
    He who stands now on death's triumphal steep,
    Awakened out of life wherein we sleep
And dream of what he knows and sees, being dead.
But never death for him was dark or dread:
    'Look forth' he bade the soul, and fear not. Weep,
    All ye that trust not in his truth, and keep
Vain memory's vision of a vanished head
As all that lives of all that once was he
Save that which lightens from his word: but we,
    Who, seeing the sunset-coloured waters roll,
Yet know the sun subdued not of the sea,
    Nor weep nor doubt that still the spirit is whole,
    And life and death but shadows of the soul.

ALLEN TATE
Sonnet to Beauty

The wonder of light is your familiar tale,
Pert wench, down to the nineteenth century:
Mr. Rimbaud the Frenchman's apostasy
Asserts the argument that you are stale,
Flat and unprofitable, importunate but pale,
Lithe Corpse! His defect of philosophy
Impugned, but could not strip your entity
Of light. Broken, our twilit visions fail.

Beauty, the doctrine of the incorporate Word
Conceives your fame; how else should you subsist?
The present age, beak southward, flies like a bird—
For often at Church I've seen the stained high glass
Pour out the Virgin and Saints, twist and untwist
The mortal youth of Christ astride an ass.

Crowned

I wear a crown invisible and clear,
    And go my lifted royal way apart
    Since you have crowned me softly in your heart
With love that is half ardent, half austere;
And as a queen disguised might pass anear
    The bitter crowd that barters in a mart,
    Veiling her pride while tears of pity start,
I hide my glory thru a jealous fear.
My crown shall stay a sweet and secret thing
Kept pure with prayer at evensong and morn,
    And when you come to take it from my head,
    I shall not weep, nor will a word be said,
But I shall kneel before you, oh my king,
    And bind my brow forever with a thorn.

ALFRED TENNYSON

The Kraken

Below the thunders of the upper deep;
Far, far beneath in the abysmal sea,
His ancient, dreamless, uninvaded sleep
The Kraken sleepeth: faintest sunlights flee
About his shadowy sides: above him swell
Huge sponges of millennial growth and height;
And far away into the sickly light,
From many a wondrous grot and secret cell
Unnumbered and enormous polypi
Winnow with giant arms the slumbering green.
There hath he lain for ages and will lie
Battening upon huge seaworms in his sleep,
Until the latter fire shall heat the deep;
Then once by man and angels to be seen,
In roaring he shall rise and on the surface die.

If I Should Ever by Chance

If I should ever by chance grow rich
I'll buy Codham, Cockridden, and Childerditch,
Roses, Pyrgo, and Lapwater,
And let them all to my elder daughter.
The rent I shall ask of her will be only
Each year's first violets, white and lonely,
The first primroses and orchises—
She must find them before I do, that is.
But if she finds a blossom on furze
Without rent they shall all for ever be hers,
Whenever I am sufficiently rich:
Codham, Cockridden, and Childerditch,
Roses, Pyrgo and Lapwater,—
I shall give them all to my elder daughter.

DYLAN THOMAS

Among Those Killed in the Dawn Raid Was a Man Aged a Hundred

When the morning was waking over the war
He put on his clothes and stepped out and he died,
The locks yawned loose and a blast blew them wide,
He dropped where he loved on the burst pavement stone
And the funeral grains of the slaughtered floor.
Tell his street on its back he stopped a sun
And the craters of his eyes grew springshoots and fire
When all the keys shot from the locks, and rang.
Dig no more for the chains of his gray-haired heart.
The heavenly ambulance drawn by a wound
Assembling waits for the spade's ring on the cage.
O keep his bones away from the common cart,
The morning is flying on the wings of his age
And a hundred storks perch on the sun's right hand.

November Cotton Flower

Boll-weevil's coming, and the winter's cold,
Made cotton-stalks look rusty, seasons old,
And cotton, scarce as any southern snow,
Was vanishing; the branch, so pinched and slow,
Failed in its function as the autumn rake;
Drouth fighting soil had caused the soil to take
All water from the streams; dead birds were found
In wells a hundred feet below the ground—
Such was the season when the flower bloomed.
Old folks were startled, and it soon assumed
Significance. Superstition saw
Something it had never seen before:
Brown eyes that loved without a trace of fear,
Beauty so sudden for that time of year.

NATASHA TRETHEWEY
Native Guard

*If this war is to be forgotten, I ask in the name of all
things sacred what shall men remember?*

FREDERICK DOUGLASS

November 1862

Truth be told, I do not want to forget
anything of my former life: the landscape's
song of bondage – dirge in the river's throat
where it churns into the Gulf, wind in trees
choked with vines. I thought to carry with me
want of freedom though I had been freed,
remembrance not constant recollection.
Yes: I was born a slave, at harvest time,
in the Parish of Ascension; I've reached
thirty-three with history of one younger
inscribed upon my back. I now use ink
to keep record, a closed book, not the lure
of memory – flawed, changeful – that dulls the lash
for the master, sharpens it for the slave.

December 1862

For the slave, having a master sharpens
the bend into work, the way the sergeant
moves us now to perfect battalion drill,
dress parade. Still, we're called supply units –
not infantry – and so we dig trenches,
haul burdens for the army no less heavy
than before. I heard the colonel call it
nigger work. Half rations make our work
familiar still. We take those things we need
from the Confederates' abandoned homes:
salt, sugar, even this journal, near full
with someone else's words, overlapped now,
crosshatched beneath mine. On every page,
his story intersecting with my own.

January 1863

O how history intersects – my own
berth upon a ship called the *Northern Star*
and I'm delivered into a new life,
Fort Massachusetts: a great irony –
both path and destination of freedom
I'd not dared to travel. Here, now, I walk
ankle-deep in sand, fly-bitten, nearly
smothered by heat, and yet I can look out
upon the Gulf and see the surf breaking,
tossing the ships, the great gunboats bobbing
on the water. And are we not the same,
slaves in the hands of the master, destiny?
– night sky red with the promise of fortune,
dawn pink as new flesh: healing, unfettered.

January 1863

Today, dawn red as warning. Unfettered
supplies, stacked on the beach at our landing,
washed away in the storm that rose too fast,
caught us unprepared. Later, as we worked,
I joined in the low singing someone raised
to pace us, and felt a bond in labor
I had not known. It was then a dark man
removed his shirt, revealed the scars, crosshatched
like the lines in this journal, on his back.
It was he who remarked at how the ropes
cracked like whips on the sand, made us take note
of the wild dance of a tent loosed by wind.
We watched and learned. Like any shrewd master,
we know now to tie down what we will keep.

February 1863

We know it is our duty now to keep
white men as prisoners – rebel soldiers,
would-be masters. We're all bondsmen here, each
to the other. Freedom has gotten them
captivity. For us, a conscription
we have chosen – jailors to those who still
would have us slaves. They are cautious, dreading
the sight of us. Some neither read nor write,
are laid too low and have few words to send
but those I give them. Still, they are wary
of a negro writing, taking down letters.
X binds them to the page – a mute symbol
like the cross on a grave. I suspect they fear
I'll listen, put something else down in ink.

March 1863

I listen, put down in ink what I know
they labor to say between silences
too big for words: worry for beloveds –
My Dearest, how are you getting along –
what has become of their small plots of land –
did you harvest enough food to put by?
They long for the comfort of former lives –
I see you as you were, waving goodbye.
Some send photographs – a likeness in case
the body can't return. Others dictate
harsh facts of this war: *The hot air carries*
the stench of limbs, rotten in the bone pit.
Flies swarm – a black cloud. We hunger, grow weak.
When men die, we eat their share of hardtack.

April 1863

When men die, we eat their share of hardtack
trying not to recall their hollow sockets,
the worm-stitch of their cheeks. Today we buried
the last of our dead from Pascagoula,
and those who died retreating to our ship –
white sailors in blue firing upon us
as if we were the enemy. I'd thought
the fighting over, then watched a man fall
beside me, knees-first as in prayer, then
another, his arms outstretched as if borne
upon the cross. Smoke that rose from each gun
seemed a soul departing. The Colonel said:
an unfortunate incident; said:
their names shall deck the page of history.

June 1863

Some names shall deck the page of history
as it is written on stone. Some will not.
Yesterday, word came of colored troops, dead
on the battlefield at Port Hudson; how
General Banks was heard to say *I have*
no dead there, and left them, unclaimed. Last night,
I dreamt their eyes still open – dim, clouded
as the eyes of fish washed ashore, yet fixed –
staring back at me. Still, more come today
eager to enlist. Their bodies – haggard
faces, gaunt limbs – bring news of the mainland.
Starved, they suffer like our prisoners. Dying,
they plead for what we do not have to give.
Death makes equals of us all: a fair master.

August 1864

Dumas was a fair master to us all.
He taught me to read and write: I was a man-
servant, if not a man. At my work,
I studied natural things – all manner
of plants, birds I draw now in my book: wren,
willet, egret, loon. Tending the gardens,
I thought only to study live things, thought
never to know so much about the dead.
Now I tend Ship Island graves, mounds like dunes
that shift and disappear. I record names,
send home simple notes, not much more than how
and when – an official duty. I'm told
it's best to spare most detail, but I know
there are things which must be accounted for.

1865

These are things which must be accounted for:
slaughter under the white flag of surrender –
black massacre at Fort Pillow; our new name,
the Corps d'Afrique – words that take the *native*
from our claim; mossbacks and freedmen – exiles
in their own homeland; the diseased, the maimed,
every lost limb, and what remains: phantom
ache, memory haunting an empty sleeve;
the hog-eaten at Gettysburg, unmarked
in their graves; all the dead letters, unanswered;
untold stories of those that time will render
mute. Beneath battlefields, green again,
the dead molder – a scaffolding of bone
we tread upon, forgetting. Truth be told.

CÉSAR VALLEJO

Testimony

I will die in Paris, on a day the rain's been coming down hard,
a day I can even now recall.
I will die in Paris—I try not to take this too much to heart—
on a Thursday, probably, in the Fall.
It'll be like today, a Thursday: a Thursday on which, as I make
and remake this poem, the very bones
in my forearms ache.
Never before, along the road, have I felt more alone.
César Vallejo is dead: everyone used to knock him about,
they'll say, though he'd done no harm;
they hit him hard with a rod
and, also, a length of rope; this will be borne out
by Thursdays, by the bones in his forearms,
by loneliness, by heavy rain, by the aforementioned roads.

translated by Paul Muldoon

PAUL VERLAINE & ARTHUR RIMBAUD
Arsehole

A self-effacing mauve carnation, crimped
and crouching in moss,
it seems, after lovemaking, somewhat lachrymose,
white buttocks fleeing towards the heart of its rim.

There's a weeping of threadlike droplets of cream
a cruel wind will dismiss
till they lose themselves in a beckoning mass
of clots and red marl grume.

In dreams, my mouth is a cupping glass to its bubo.
My soul, bent on straight-up houghmagandie,
writes it off as a tear-pit, its twitch after little twitch.

It's a fitful olive-brown, a pipe
from which pours such heavenly candy:
a Promised Land complete with an irrigation ditch.

translated by Paul Muldoon

ELLEN BRYANT VOIGT

[Thought at first that grief had brought him down.]

Thought at first that grief had brought him down.
His wife dead, his own hand dug the grave
under a willow oak, in family ground—
he got home sick, was dead when morning came.

By week's end, his cousin who worked in town
was seized at once by fever and by chill,
left his office, walked back home at noon,
death ripening in him like a boil.

Soon it was a farmer in the field—
someone's brother, someone's father—
left the mule in its traces and went home.
Then the mason, the miller at his wheel,
from deep in the forest the hunter, the logger,
and the sun still up everywhere in the kingdom.

Childhood

When I was a child I knew red miners
dressed raggedly and wearing carbide lamps.
I saw them come down red hills to their camps
dyed with red dust from old Ishkooda mines.
Night after night I met them on the roads,
or on the streets in town I caught their glance;
the swing of dinner buckets in their hands,
and grumbling undermining all their words.

I also lived in low cotton country
where moonlight hovered over ripe haystacks,
or stumps of trees, and croppers' rotting shacks
with famine, terror, flood, and plague near by;
where sentiment and hatred still held sway
and only bitter land was washed away.

JOHN GREENLEAF WHITTIER

To a Cape Ann Schooner

Luck to the craft that bears this name of mine,
Good fortune follow with her golden spoon
The glazèd hat and tarry pantaloon;
And wheresoe'er her keel shall cut the brine,
Cod, hake and haddock quarrel for her line.
Shipped with her crew, whatever wind may blow,
Or tides delay, my wish with her shall go,
Fishing by proxy. Would that it might show
At need her course, in lack of sun and star,
Where icebergs threaten, and the sharp reefs are;
Lift the blind fog on Anticosti's lee
And Avalon's rock; make populous the sea
Round Grand Manan with eager finny swarms,
Break the long calms, and charm away the storms.

RICHARD WILBUR

Sonnet

The winter deepening, the hay all in,
The barn fat with cattle, the apple-crop
Conveyed to market or the fragrant bin,
He thinks the time has come to make a stop,

And sinks half-grudging in his firelit seat,
Though with his heavy body's full consent,
In what would be the posture of defeat,
But for that look of rigorous content.

Outside, the night dives down like one great crow
Against his cast-off clothing where it stands
Up to the knees in miles of hustled snow,

Flapping and jumping like a kind of fire,
And floating skyward its abandoned hands
In gestures of invincible desire.

ELLA WHEELER WILCOX

The Sonnet

Alone it stands in Poesy's fair land,
   A temple by the muses set apart;
   A perfect structure of consummate art,
By artists builded and by genius planned.
Beyond the reach of the apprentice hand,
   Beyond the ken of the untutored heart,
   Like a fine carving in a common mart,
Only the favored few will understand.
A *chef-d'oeuvre* toiled over with great care,
   Yet which the unseeing careless crowd goes by,
A plainly set, but well-cut solitaire,
An ancient bit of pottery, too rare
   To please or hold aught save the special eye,
These only with the sonnet can compare.

OSCAR WILDE

On the Sale by Auction of Keats' Love Letters

These are the letters which Endymion wrote
To one he loved in secret, and apart.
And now the brawlers of the auction mart
Bargain and bid for each poor blotted note,
Ay! for each separate pulse of passion quote
The merchant's price. I think they love not art
Who break the crystal of a poet's heart
That small and sickly eyes may glare and gloat.
Is it not said that many years ago,
In a far Eastern town, some soldiers ran
With torches through the midnight, and began
To wrangle for mean raiment, and to throw
Dice for the garments of a wretched man,
Not knowing the God's wonder, or His woe?

WILLIAM WORDSWORTH

Nuns fret not at their convent's narrow room

Nuns fret not at their convent's narrow room;
And hermits are contented with their cells;
And students with their pensive citadels;
Maids at the wheel, the weaver at his loom,
Sit blithe and happy; bees that soar for bloom,
High as the highest Peak of Furness-fells,
Will murmur by the hour in foxglove bells:
In truth the prison, unto which we doom
Ourselves, no prison is: and hence for me,
In sundry moods, 'twas pastime to be bound
Within the Sonnet's scanty plot of ground;
Pleased if some Souls (for such there needs must be)
Who have felt the weight of too much liberty,
Should find brief solace there, as I have found.

LADY MARY WROTH

from *A Crowne of Sonetts Dedicated to Love*

I

In this strange labyrinth how shall I turn?
    Ways are on all sides while the way I miss:
    If to the right hand, there in love I burn;
    Let me go forward, therein danger is;

If to the left, suspicion hinders bliss,
    Let me turn back, shame cries I ought return
    Nor faint though crosses with my fortune kiss;
    Stand still is harder, although sure to mourn;

Thus let me take the right, or left hand way;
    Go forward, or stand still, or back retire;
    I must these doubts endure without allay
    Or help, but travail find for my best hire;

Yet that which most my troubled sense doth move
Is to leave all, and take the thread of love.

Who so list to hounte I know where is an hynde

Who so list to hounte I know where is an hynde;
    But as for me, helas, I may no more:
    The vayne travaill hath weried me so sore,
    I ame of theim that farthest cometh behinde;
Yet may I by no meanes my weried mynde
    Drawe from the Diere: but as she fleeth afore
    Faynting I folowe; I leve off therefore,
    Sithens in a nett I seke to hold the wynde.
Who list her hount I put him owte of dowbte,
    As well as I may spend his tyme in vain:
    And graven with Diamondes in letters plain
    There is written her faier neck rounde abowte:
    'Noli me tangere for Cesars I ame,
    And wylde for to hold though I seme tame.'

ELINOR WYLIE

Sonnet

You are the faintest freckles on the hide
Of fawns; the hoofprint stamped into the slope
Of slithering glaciers by the antelope;
The silk upon the mushroom's under side
Constricts you, and your eyelashes are wide
In pools uptilted on the hills; you grope
For swings of water twisted to a rope
Over a ledge where amber pebbles glide.

Shelley perceived you on the Caucasus;
Blake prisoned you in glassy grains of sand
And Keats in goblin jars from Samarcand;
Poor Coleridge found you in a poppy-seed;
But you escape the clutching most of us,
Shaped like a ghost, and imminent with speed.

WILLIAM BUTLER YEATS
Leda and the Swan

A sudden blow: the great wings beating still
Above the staggering girl, her thighs caressed
By the dark webs, her nape caught in his bill,
He holds her helpless breast upon his breast.

How can those terrified vague fingers push
The feathered glory from her loosening thighs?
And how can body, laid in that white rush,
But feel the strange heart beating where it lies?

A shudder in the loins engenders there
The broken wall, the burning roof and tower
And Agamemnon dead.
                             Being so caught up,
So mastered by the brute blood of the air,
Did she put on his knowledge with his power
Before the indifferent beak could let her drop?

ACKNOWLEDGEMENTS

We are grateful to the following for permission to reproduce copyright material:

W. H. AUDEN: Excerpt from *The Shield of Achilles*, Random House, 1955, copyright © The Estate of W. H. Auden, 1951 / 'The Quest IV: The Traveller' from *Collected Poems* by W. H. Auden, edited by Edward Mendelson, copyright 1939, renewed © 1967 by W. H. Auden and Christopher Isherwood, 1967. Reproduced by permission of Curtis Brown, Ltd; and Random House, an imprint and division of Penguin Random House LLC. All rights reserved

GEORGE BARKER: 'To My Mother' from *Collected Poems* by George Barker, Faber & Faber Limited, poem 292. Reproduced by permission of the publisher

JOHN BERRYMAN: 'Sonnet 13' from *Berryman's Sonnets* by John Berryman, Faber & Faber Limited, copyright © John Berryman, 1967, renewed © Kate Berryman, 1995. Reproduced by permission of Faber & Faber Limited; and Farrar, Straus and Giroux. All rights reserved

REGINALD DWAYNE BETTS: 'House of Unending', *Poetry* Magazine, April 2019. Reproduced by permission of McCormick Literary

ELIZABETH BISHOP: 'Some Dreams They Forgot' from *Complete Poems* by Elizabeth Bishop, Jonathan Cape, copyright © Alice Helen Methfessel, 1983; and *Poems* by Elizabeth Bishop, copyright © The Alice H. Methfessel Trust, 2011. Publisher's Note and compilation copyright © Farrar, Straus and Giroux, 2011. Reproduced by permission of The Random House Group Limited; and Farrar, Straus and Giroux. All rights reserved

GWENDOLYN BROOKS: 'Mentors' from *Selected Poems* by Gwendolyn Brooks, HarperCollins, 1963. Reproduced by consent of Brooks Permissions

154

INDEX OF TITLES AND FIRST LINES